THE ART OF
Persian Tea

FARAHNAZ AMIRSOLEYMANI

❀

FARI PUBLISHING

FARI PUBLISHING

Published by Fari Publishing

Copyright © 2014 by Farahnaz Amirsoleymani
All rights reserved under the Pan-American
and International Copyright Conventions.

Printed in the United States of America.
Published simultaneously in United Kingdom, and Canada.

Library of Congress Control Number: 2014904253

ISBN 978-0-615-98029-4

FIRST EDITION

Typography: Cochin, Gothic

PUBLISHER'S NOTE
The advice contained herein is for informational purposes only.
This book is not a substitute for psychological treatment, or for
medical care by a physician. The author and the publisher disclaim
any and all liability for any consequences, damages, and
outcomes (including property damage, physical injury, or death)
that may occur as resulting from the use of the information
contained in this book.

For More Information Visit:
WWW.FARIPUBLISHING.COM
WWW.FARAHNAZAMIRSOLEYMANI.COM

Contents:

Tete-a-Tete

I remember many afternoons sitting with my grandmother in the kitchen watching her blend fragrant and exquisite tea blends - using ingredients such as Persian roses, black tea from India, pomegranate seeds, orange blossoms, and cardamom to name a few. Mesmerized by the beauty of it all, I would raise the estekan (tulip-shaped glass), close my eyes, and savor each delicate note. I loved spending those precious hours alone with her, sipping tea listening to her gentle voice explaining the healing properties of each blend. Inspired by my memories I started to blend my own tea. The Art of Persian tea is an experience focusing on the senses and subtle experiences, those which effortlessly transport us elsewhere... Through a delicate fragrance, a taste, or a sight, tea infusions promote a feeling of well-being and balance.

Tea, like love has no boundaries. It's readily available everywhere and within the reach of everyone. It is simple and pure. All you need is warm water and the patience to linger a few moments while the tea leaves dance (infuse). Much like love, tea is layered and complex - it is sophisticated and mysterious. There is so much to know, so much to explore. The tea in your cup is a result of a delicious journey.

In this book, I'm thrilled to share my passion for tea along with generation's worth of family recipes and cure-alls that are truly priceless jewels. You'll find simple menu suggestions for a beautiful tea party, alongside an introduction to the Persian Ayurvedic diet: Unani, Persian customs, an in-depth profile on tea, and the secrets to blending tea.

I'm delighted to invite you into the celebration of love, life, culture, and tantalizing flavors to savor. As we say in Persian, Noush'e Jan!

Farahnaz

Introduction To Tea In Persian Culture

The origin of tea is infused with a fine blend of fact, myth, and ancient concepts of spirituality and philosophy. According to the Chinese legend, emperor Shen Nung discovered tea accidentally in 2700BC. The legend is: after a large meal one day, Shen Nung was relaxing in the garden with a cup of boiling water. On this occasion, a fortuitous blunder caused a few dry leaves to accidentally fall into his cup - unnoticed he consumed the drink. The emperor enjoyed drinking the infused water as it had a most unusual and delicious flavour. He felt so immensely invigorated and refreshed, Shen Nung set out to further research the plant whereby he discovered tea to possess medicinal properties, and thereby invented tea.

For several hundred years tea was at first seen as a therapeutic drink under the Western Han dynasty (206BC – 24 AD). During this time tea plants were quite limited and only consumed by royalty. Under the Eastern Han period of the dynasty, tea became a daily part of the emperors and aristocratic people's lives. However, it was only under the Tang dynasty (618 AD- 907 AD) that tea became more widely available, and began to show significance in Chinese tradition thanks to a scholar named Lu Yu who published the first definitive book on tea: *Cha Ching* or *The Tea Classic*. Lu Yu documentation of his knowledge of tea, gave tea a identity to mainstream China. Thus the art of tea was born.

Tea was first introduced to Iran at the end of the 15th century. It owes its development to the difficulty of importing coffee into Iran: which was greatly enjoyed at the time, but very hard to obtain from the producing countries. Tea gradually began to replace coffee, as it was easily attainable throught the Slik Road. At this time Tea houses, or chaikhanehs gained prominence.

It was not until the end of the 19th century that the first attempt was made to cultivate the tea plant (Camellia Sinensis) in Lahijan, a region in the northern province of Gilan in Iran, and not until the beginning of the 20th century that the first crop of Iranian tea was sold on the local market. Today Iran is the eighth largest producer of tea in the world and consumes almost its entire output of tea.

Iranians are great tea drinkers. Tea or "chai" is the national beverage – I would even say the national pastime or obsession. Tea is served virtually everywhere from mosques to bazaars, and of course at homes all through the day. The taking of tea is a ritual unto itself: all social gatherings, meetings, or formal & non-formal occasions will begin with the offering of tea, and most meals will end with it. In fact, it is an insult not to offer someone tea; the insulted Iranian will think, "Yek chai taarof nakard!" - "S/He didn't even offer me tea!"

At chaikhaneh (Tea houses), tea is served after a meal, it is rarely served before or during a meal. Some chaikhanehs have takhts (a low-rise platforms covered in rugs and pillows) at which one sits.

Tea in Iran is traditionally prepared in a samovar (a large metal heating vessel originally from Russia), and then poured into elegant tulip-shaped glasses called estekans atop of a saucer. Many people (mostly men or children) pour the tea in the saucer, and drink it from there - since there is more surface area, the tea cools quicker this way. The tea of choice in Iran almost always is a loose-leaf black tea, and herbal infusions (tisanes). The color, strength, and appearance of tea is very important: tea is served either por rang or kam rang – light or dark. Tea is traditionally never drunk with milk except on the border with Pakistan. Everywhere else tea is served plain with sugar cubes (The Iranian way is to place a sugar cube on the tongue and then drink the tea). Other tea accompaniments include: cardamom, dried limes, a slice of lemon, dates, a splash of rosewater, and or a spoonful of cherry preserves.

Throughout history, and within the cultures of the world's most ancient civilizations, tea has enjoyed tremendous popularity due to its simplicity, variety, and flavor. Moreover, through exploration, discovery and experimentation, tea has exploded into the most widely consumed beverage in the world, second to water. Tea is iconic, and the world of tea is vast, and specialized just like that of fine wine.

The Persian diet
Unani

*A*yurveda is an ancient practice of alternative medicine native to India. The first mentions of Ayurveda are made in Indian medicinal literature written around 1700 BCE. The main goal of Ayurvedic medicine is to restore health and increase longevity through the establishment of balance. Thus, practitioners of Ayurvedic medicine see imbalance as the main cause of all physical and psychological ailments. In order to treat this imbalance, practitioners of Ayurvedic medicine turn mainly to plant-based medicines and treatments that are the building blocks of the Ayurvedic diet.

Of course, it is not surprising that this form of alternative medicine spread quickly throughout the ancient world and helped influence and advance the medicinal practices of many ancient civilizations. For example, a close look at ancient Chinese medicine reveals the heavy influence of Ayurvedic medicinal practices on this form of ancient medicine. The ancient Chinese philosophy regarding the Yin and Yan nature of foods is in direct correlation to the Ayurvedic diet's emphasize on the medicinal balancing nature of certain foods. Furthermore, it's hard not to correlate the Ayurvedic notions of Vata, Pitta and Kapha with the notions of spirit, water and blood which work together to balance the flow of Qi.

Though the intricacies of Ayurvedic medicine and ancient Chinese medicine are well known throughout the western world, the heavy influence of the Ayurvedic diet and medicine upon the cuisine and medicinal practices of the ancient Persian culture is still one that requires further exploration. Like the Chinese, the Persians drew heavily upon the Ayurvedic notion of balance when fashioning their cultural cuisine and medicinal views. However, unlike the ancient Chinese whose medicinal practices advanced in the direction of the Meridian theory of pressure points and flows of energy, the Ancient Persian's medicinal practices advanced in the art of "Ishoku Dogen" which means, "Food is medicine and medicine is food".

In keeping with the philosophy of "Ishoku Dogen" the Persian food culture evolved to treat food as a source of disease prevention. In keeping with the Ayurvedic principles, the early Persian physicians, and philosophers such as: Hakim Ibn Sina (also know as Avicenna) developed an intricate system (Unani) of combining foods based on the categorizations of four humors: cold, hot, dry, and moist. The description 'hot' or 'cold' doesn't relate to the temperature of food but rather to the effect - food has on the body.

All food is broken down by enzymes in the stomach: consequently this effects the bodies cells and ultimately how the body functions. Enzymes react to the 'hot' and 'cold' food. For example, a 'cold' food like an orange slows down the digestive process, which in turn slows the body down. On the other hand, 'hot' foods like spices speeds up the digestive process, and increases the

15

bodies metabolic rate.

A persons diet is also determined by season, and where they live and the climate. This is where the humors 'dry' and 'moist' come to play. So if someone lives in a dry area they need to consume moist foods, and if you live in a moist environment you need dry foods – in means of keeping balance. Also according to Unani practices people must also eat seasonally – meaning buying local organic ingredients (farm to table), and buying food seasonally (natural harvest time).

This system of food combination was designed to help maintain balance within the body and thus ward off various physical and mental ailments brought on by imbalance within the body's natural flow.

This ancient philosophy of combining foods based on their categorization of Unani is an integral part of Persian culture and is still currently being practiced. However, what sets Unani apart from the Ayurvedic diet developed in India is the fact that the Unani diet includes both white and red meats, as well as other animal products, into its categorization. This is not surprising, given the fact that the Persian diet is a semi-vegetarian diet, with close ties to the Mediterranean diet. As follows is a list of 'hot' and 'cold' foods. Please note: this book is vegetarian. However, I categorized meats on their 'hot' and 'cold' properties for knowledge bases only.

Garmi

(Hot Foods)

Apples, bananas, carrots, caviar, chicken, chickpeas, dried fruits (all), eggs, figs, garlic, herbs (except parsley & coriander), lamb, nuts (all sorts), olives, onions, quince, radishes, rosewater, spices (except sumac), vinegar, wheat, honey.

Sardi

(Cold Foods)

All unripe fruit, all fresh fruit (except apples, quince, figs, & bananas), all vegetables (except carrots, radish, okra, onions, garlic, red & green peppers), beef, coffee, dairy products, lentils, rice, sugar, sumac, verjuice.

Bi Taraf

(Neutral Foods)

Feta, and tea.

Chapter 1: Persian Customs

Persian Hospitality

(Mehman Hediyeh Khodast)

Hospitality is the core of Persian culture. In Persian culture guests are thought as a blessing from god "Mehman hediyeh kodast". When a guest enters a Persian home they are treated as royalty, they are given the best seat in the house, the best tea, the best food, and are the center of attention. It should also be noted that whenever a newcomer (guest) enters the room, all those present must stand up as a sign of respect, whether you know the person or not. If you are the newcomer (guest) entering the room, you may ask them to remain seated by saying: "befarmaid, khahesh mikonam" (please do stay seated).

Nazri

(Cooked in Honor of)

Nazri is a religious offering of tea / food to the Imans, or god - in hopes of receiving something of higher value (such as a husband, or child). Once the person's wish has been granted, they must make a special tea / food once a year on a religious day of their choice, and give this food to the needy. The tea / food of Nazri is believed to have healing powers, and brings good luck to those who eat it.

Ta'arof

(Ritual Politeness)

Ta'arof is a beautiful part of Persian culture that is deep rooted in Persian hospitality that represents being polite, gracious and humble. Ta'arof is a verbal dance between an offeror and the acceptor, that continues until either party aggres. It is customary for the acceptor not to accept the offer of the offerer until the third time.

Example of Ta'arof:
For example, a host (offeror) offers a guest a cup of tea. The acceptor (guest) politely refuses, even if they are really thirsty. The host will offer a cup of tea a second time, and the guest still politely refuses. Finally on the third time the guest will accept the cup of tea.

For some the act of ta'arof is troublesome (a waste of time), and they will say "ta'arof Nakonid" which means to stop ta'arofing.

Chapter 2: The Health Benefits of Tea

The health benefits of tea.

For over 4,700 years people have been exploring the health benefits of tea. Be it mental alertness, safeguard against disease, or rejuvenation, Nevertheless tea is a welcomed pleasure for many reasons.

As the world's most widely consumed beverage next to water, tea began not as a beverage, but as a medicine.

The research conducted on the health benefits of tea is plentiful. As more studies continue to test the outcomes of the research on human subjects, immensely valuable information is gained as to how tea can be of positive use in our individual lives.

As follows I present you with some of the most promising discoveries made to date:

Antioxidants

In response to the array of toxins and adverse influences that impact each of us on a daily basis, our bodies produce unstable molecules called "oxidants" or "free radicals" that can damage healthy cells. The outcome of these harmful influences can be chronic illnesses, damage to the immune system, organ disease, and many other health complications.

The effects of free radicals can be reduced by the naturally-occurring antioxidants found in foods such as fruits, vegetables, and tea. The antioxidants quench the free radicals so that they are unable to cause damage to other healthy cells. In this way, it is believed that antioxidants may be responsible for the reduction in the occurrence, as well as inhibiting their growth.

Below is a small glossary of terms of antioxidants found in tea. They are all very closely inter-related.

Antioxidants are molecules that slow or inhibit oxidants.

Polyphenols found to have powerful antioxidant qualities.

Flavonoids (or bioflavonoids), also collectively known as Vitamin P and citrin, are a class of a type of polyphenol found in tea.

Catechins are a component of flavonoids, and are found in the tea plant Camellia sinensis. There are four types of catechins that exist in tea, with EGCG (epigallocatechin gallate) being the one most often discussed with regards to tea's health benefits.

How tea aids our bodies..

Sustainable Energy
All teas contain caffeine (or theine). However, the caffeine present in tea is different from that found in coffee. It stimulates the nervous system in a slow and progressive way. It helps you to feel awake and concentrated in a sustainable way.

Mental Clarity
The amino acids that exist in tea may aid in creating a calm, yet more alert, mental state. This effect can continue for three to four hours.

Immune System
Antioxidants may aid in the safeguard of the immune system. The amino acid L-theanine present in tea may "prime" the immune system to help it prepare to fight infection, bacteria, viruses and fungi. Additionally, tea is plentiful in vitamins and minerals including B1, B2, B6, C, folic acid, magnesium, potassium and zinc.

Beauty from the inside
Some of the benefits to heart health that have been indicated by research studies include lowering LDL cholesterol2 and boosting the ability of blood vessel lining to expand upon increased blood flow. It is also believed that tea might also aid in the lowering of blood pressure, and combating cholesterol. Tea also has a large amount of vitamin B complex (especially vitamin B9) which helps our body to maintain general wellbeing.

Beauty from the outside:

Tea is also rich in vitamins, notably vitamin P that helps strengthen hair, tea fights free radicals and helps to prevent acne, and is a delicious, soothing way to promote healthy skin.

A Health Smile:

Tea contains a natural fluoride, promoting healthy tooth enamel, and the flavonoids in tea may reduce the formation of plaque by bacteria in the mouth.

329

Chapter 3:
Tea
Exploration

Tea Profile

Camellia Sinensis

All true teas—black, green, white or oolong come from the same plant: Camellia Sinensis. While the tea products differ, the leaves are virtually the same. Camellia Sinensis is a evergreen and grows in hot, humid climates where there is plenty of sunshine and lots of rain. A tea plant can grow up to 10m to 15m high. However, to make it easier to harvest, tea plants are usually cropped to 1.10m high and maintained at this height. The life of the average tea plant is around forty years, however it has been known for certain varieties to live for 100 years. The tea plants are harvested several times a year and are harvested by hand. The harvesting technique and the season of the harvest changes according to each country. Each harvesting period gives the tea a different flavour: for example a springtime harvest will not taste the same as a summertime harvest. After the fresh Camellia Sinensis leaves are processed and their exposure to oxygen will determine their final classification. All other botanical beverages not containing Camellia Sinensis are called tisanes: herbal and rooibos infusions. Persian's traditionally favor black tea, green tea, and herbal infusions. While white tea, and rooibos are seldom ever used. As follows is an in-depth profile on the different types of teas...

Black Tea:

(Cha'i Siyah)

Black tea is a result of the complete oxidation of the Camellia Sinensis leaf. First produced in China, the tea increased in popularity when the British cultivated the plant in India, Sri Lanka, and Africa. First the leaf is spread out and left to wither (wilt), losing some moisture, stiffness and much of it's weight. Then rolled, exposing essential oils to air and starting the oxidization process. When this is complete the leaf is heated to stop the process, graded for quality and packed. Black teas are known for their robust, full-bodied flavors of cocoa, earth, molasses, and honey. Black tea is the most common tea enjoyed by Persians. Examples of black tea include: Assam, Ceylon, and many others.

Green Tea

Green tea is an unoxidized tea, green tea is picked and quickly heated by steaming or pan frying. The goodness of the leaf is sealed inside. The most well-known greens come from China and Japan. The flavors are grassy, vegetal, nutty, and sweet. Because the leaf is so delicate, the tea should be brewed in water that is well below boiling to prevent cooking the leaves and destroying the subtle notes of the tea. Examples of green tea include: gunpowder green tea, jasmine pearl, sencha, and many others.

Oolong Tea:
(Cha'i Oolong)

Oolong tea sometimes referred to as semi-fermented tea is oxidized and often rolled after picking, allowing the essential oils to react with the air. This process turns the leaf darker and produces distinctive fragrances before heat is added to set the taste. The resulting tea can be anywhere between a green and a black tea, depending on the processing method. Oolongs can be recognized by their large leaves and a complexity of flavor that ranges from highly floral and intensely fruity to mildly roasted with honey nuances. Oolong tea has less caffeine, making it an idea drink for the afternoon or the evening. Examples of oolong tea include: orchid oolong.

White Tea

(Cha'i Sefid)

White tea is minimally processed; it is generally only picked and air dried. The highest-quality white teas are picked early in the spring before the leaf buds have opened and while still covered with silky, white hair. The traditional varietals used for white tea have abundant downy hair on the young leaf shoots. These delicate teas have clear flavors that tend toward savory, nutty, and vegetal. Traditionally harvested in China, they are the focus of many studies on health benefits for their high levels of antioxidants. Examples of White tea include: silver needle, and high grade white tea.

Herbal Infusions:

(Cha'i Araqiyat)

Herbal infusions, or tisanes (a French word), are not teas. They are usually made from dried flowers, fruits, and or herbs, and they do not contain any caffeine. Traditionally tisanes are made and consumed for homeopathic cures, boasting a astounding array of benefits from serenity – to rejuvenation. Please keep in mind that almost all flowers, fruit, and or herbs can be made into a tisane. Examples of tisanes include: lemon verbena, chamomile, rooibos, lavender, and mint.

Red Tea (Rooibos)

(Cha'i Ghermez

Red tea also known as rooibos - is a type of herbal infusion and is a caffeine-free herb grown only in South Africa in the Cederberg mountains, to the north of Capetown. It is rich in Super Oxide Dismustase (SOD), an outstanding anti-oxidant. It contains many minerals promoting calm & relaxing properties. It is known to alleviate insomnia, nervous tension, mild depression & nausea. Good for the digestion, rooibos is smooth, mellow & marvellous.

Tea Grading

The value of a tea is determined by its grade, which relates to the fineness of the harvest and the size of the tea leaf.

In the typology of grades, the word Orange is used; it originates from the Dutch royal family Oranje Nassau, and does not refer to the fruit.

- Whole leaves

- Broken leaves
    - B.O.P. Broken Orange Pekoe: the leaf is no longer whole it is smaller than in the O.P. This creates a darker, stronger infusion

    - F.B.O.P. Flowery Broken Orange Pekoe
    - G.B.O.P. Golden Broken Orange Pekoe
    - T.G.B.O.P. Tippy Golden Broken Orange Pekoe

- Ground leaves
    - F. Fannings: the pieces are flat and smaller than in the B.O.P, this creates a very strong infusion
    - D. Dust: finely ground, the leaves are only used for certain kinds of tea bags.

Flower
Orange Pekoe

Pekoe

Orange
Pekoe

Second
Souchong

Pekoe
Souchong

Chapter 4:
Persian Tea Cabinet - The Essentials

Tea Cabinet – The Essentials

Here is the list of the essential teas, dried herbs, spices and flowers used in preparing Persian tea. When buying dried flowers, essential oils & extracts – please ensure all items are food grade, and store items in airtight containers in a cool, dark place away from the kitchen stove. Please note: only buy organic ingredients, and use loose-leaf teas, herbs, and spices within six months of opening.

Black Teas (Chai Siyah):
> Assam Black Tea
> Ceylon Black Tea

Green Tea (Chai Sabz):
> Gunpowder Green Tea
> Jasmine Pearl Green Tea
> Monkey Picked Green Tea
> Sencha Green Tea
> Matcha Green Tea

Oolong Tea (Chai Oolong)
> Fine Oolong Tea

White Tea (Chai Sefid)
> High Grade White Tea
> Silver Needle White Tea

Dried Herbs
Dried Spearmint (Na'na)
Dried Lemon Balm (Badrang Buye)
Dried Lemon Verbrna (Behlimu)
Dried Red Rooibos (Chai Rooibos)
Dried Mulberry Leaf (Barg'e Tut)

Spices
Allspice (Felfe'e Bahareh)
Green Cardamom (Hel)
Ceylon Cinnamon (Darchin)
Cloves (Mikhak)
Dried Ginger root pieces (Zanjebil)
Nutmeg (Jowz'e Hendi)
Star Anise (Badian'e Khatai)
Saffron (Za'feran)
Peppercorns (Felfel'e Siyah)

Organic Essential Oils & Extract
Bergamot Essential Oil (Baderang)
Pure Vanilla Extract (Osareh Vanil)

Dried Flowers, Furits, Nuts, & Other
Chamomile Flowers (Babuneh)
Chrysanthemum (Gol'e Davudi)
Rose Petals (Gol'e Sorkh)
Rosehip
Dried Hibiscus Flowers (Gol'e Bamieh)
Dried Lotus Flower (Gol'e Niloofar)
Dried Marigold Petals (Gol'e Hamisheh Bahar)
Dried Lavender (Austokhodus)
Dried Jasmine (Gol'e Yas)
Borage Flowers (Gol Gab Zabun)
Dried Pistachios (Pesteh)
Bee Pollen (Zanbur Garde)
Dried Cherries (Gilas)

Tea-Compliments

Rose Water (Golab)

Orange Blossom Water (Ab Bahar Narenj)

Raw Organic Honey (Asal)

Quince Preserves (Moraba'ye Beh)
   see page 168.

Sour Cherry Preserves (Moraba'ye Albalu)
   see page 169.

Rose Petal Preserves (Moraba'ye Gol'e Sorkh)
   see page 170.

Dainty Sugared Almonds (Noghl)
   see page 160.

Sugar Cubes (Ghand)

Dried Lime (Limu Omani)

Rock Candy Sticks (Nabat)

Persian Sugar Plum (Poolaki)

Chapter 5: Methods For Brewing Tea

The Perfect Cup

There are many discussions about the best way to steep tea – some will argue that in order to fully appreciate the 'agony' of the leaves, the tea should be steeped directly in the teapot without infusors. However, I prefer to use a infusor (large enough to let the tea leaves dance - infuse freely). I myself use a clear glass teapot with built-in Infuser - this allows you to enjoy a great cup of tea with a much easier cleaning process.

Please note when infusing tea there are 4 elements to making the perfect cup of tea:

Tea Leaf
Quality & freshness matter.

The Water
Quality - use fresh cold filtered water.

The Vessel
Glass teapots are the best (flavors do not cling to glass), ceramic is great, and metal can give an unwanted flavor.

Time
key to getting the perfect balance in flavor and tannins is steeping tea to the perfect time.

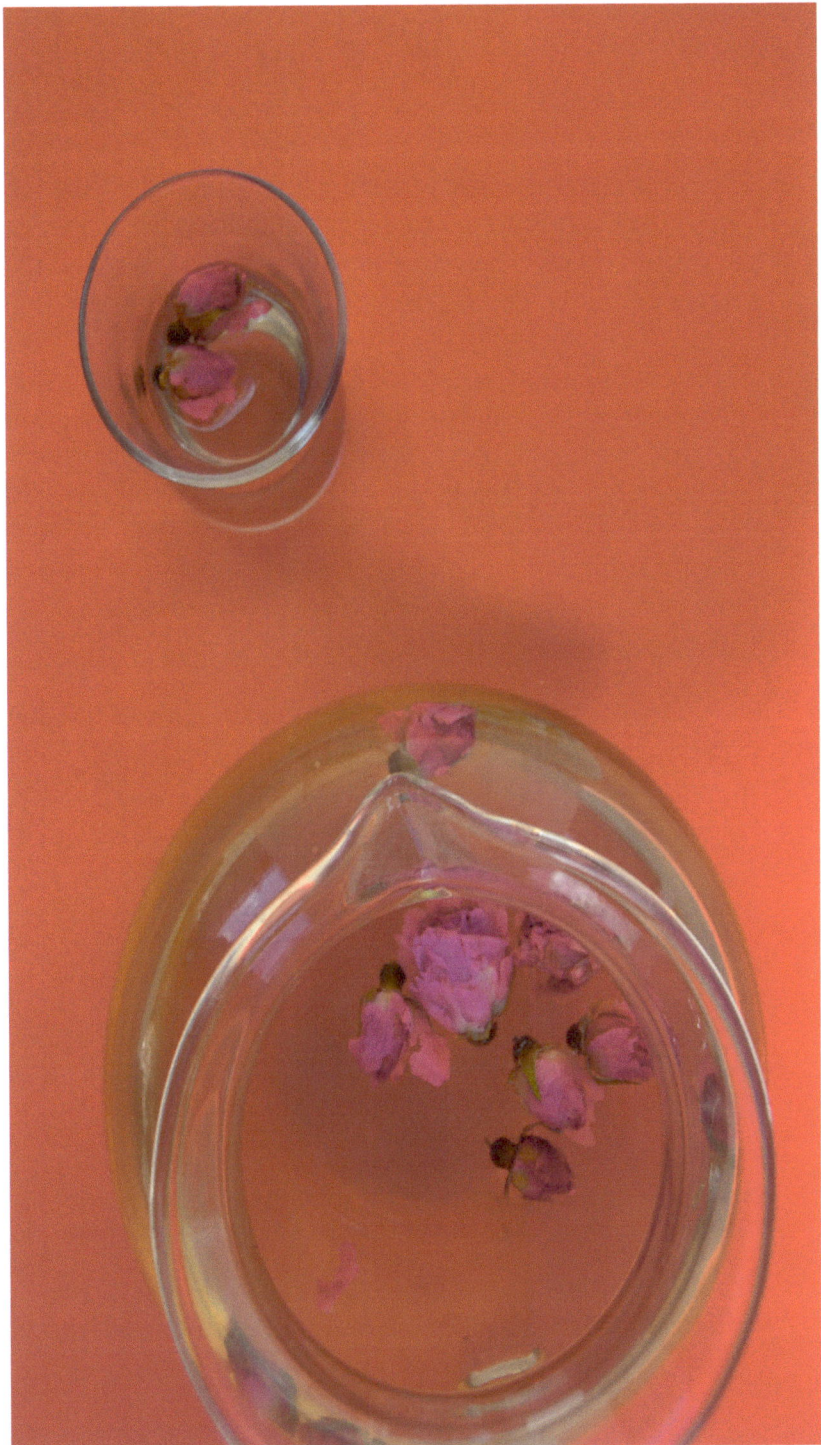

Brewing Tea

1. In a teakettle bring freshly drawn cold water to a boil. Next warm a small teapot by pouring a small amount of boiled water from the teakettle, swirl water around, and pour it out.

2. Place 1-2 teaspoons of loose-leaf tea (depending on how strong you like your tea) into the infuser / teapot, and fill teapot half way with boiling water. Cover, and Let the tea steep according to chart. (Remember to vary the time according to taste, not color. Over steeping does not contribute to flavor, only bitterness.) If you are using a samovar, steep the tea on top of the samovar.

3. Serve the tea by filling each glass halfway with tea, and add boiling water from the kettle to dilute the tea to desired strength, and serve with your favorite tea compliments.

Here is a list of some Persian tea-compliments:
rose water, orange blossom water, raw organic honey, quince preserves (see page 168), sour cherry preserves (see page 169), rose petal preserves (see page 170), dried lime, dainty sugared almonds (see page 160), sugar cubes, rock candy sticks, milk or milk alternatives (customary only on the Iran-Pakistan border), Persian sugar plum (Poolaki).

I personaly drink plain black tea with a splash of rose water, a dizzle of raw organic honey, and or a spoon of sour cherry preserves. I like my spiced based teas with almond milk, and I drink green tea, white teas, & tisanes with honey, a slice of lemon or dried lime (Limu Omani). I encourage you to try and taste different tea-compliments along with your tea - as it adds new depth, and flavor profiles to your cup.

TEA TYPE:	TIME:	TEMPERATURE:
WHITE TEA	1-4 MINUTES	STEAMING (150 - 180° F)
GREEN TEA	1-4 MINUTES	STEAMING (150 - 180° F)
OOLONG TEA	1-3 MINUTES	LIGHT BOIL (165 - 190° F)
BLACK TEA	2-5 MINUTES	ROLLING BOIL (210° F)
HEBARL TEA	5-7 MINUTES	ROLLING BOIL (210° F)
ROOIBOS TEA	5-7 MINUTES	ROLLING BOIL (210° F)

Ice Tea:

When making iced tea, follow the above method, let tea set to room temperature, and then dilute tea over ice.

Chapter 6:
The Art Of
Blending
Tea (Chai)

Blending Tea

The art of blending tea is about experimentation and creativity. Tea blending, much like tea drinking engages all the senses, so it is important to familiarize yourself with a vast amount of ingredients (teas, herbs, spices and botanicals) learn there intended scent's, and flavor profiles. When starting to blend your own tea the most important thing to know is that all great tea blends are created by trial and error – so experiment! Moreover I find it helpful to keep a tasting notebook to record the tea blends that work, and don't work. As follows are my treasured blends, these blends will highlight the distinct qualities of tea, and I hope they inspire you to create your own unique signature blends. Please note these blends can be halved or doubled

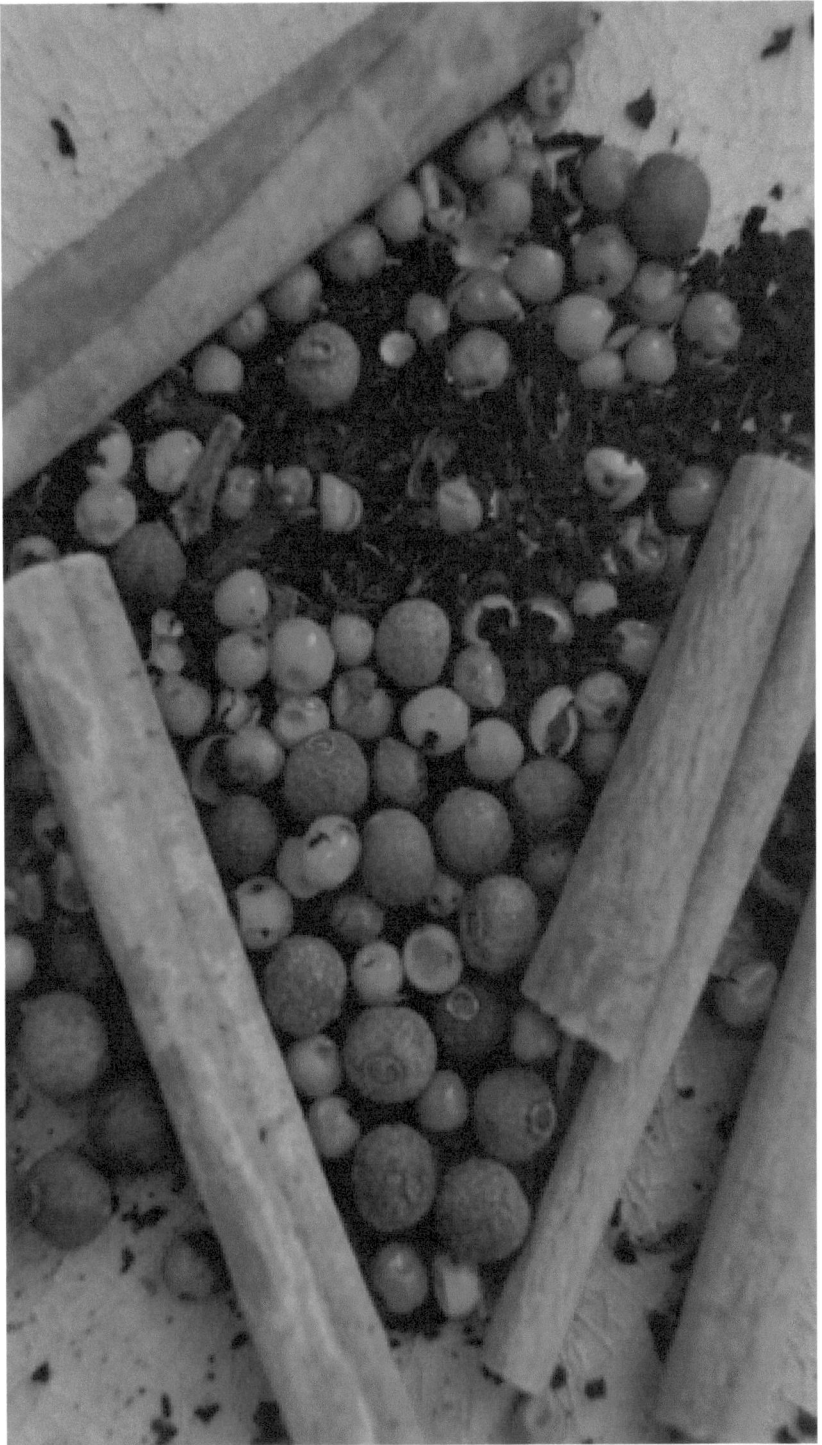

Tea Blends

Black Tea Blends

Classic Persian Tea, 60
Persian Rose, 62
Namaste Chai, 64
Grand Bazaar, 66
Turkish Apple, 68
Cozy Monkey, 70
Tabriz Beauty, 72
Lover's Tea, 74

Green Tea Blends:

Salam (Hello), 78
Enlighten Mint, 80
Whirling Dervish, 82
Sabzi, 84
Beauty Tea, 86
Aroosi, 88
Magnificent, 90

Oolong Tea Blends:

Rumi Tea, 94
Imperial Label, 96
Rock & Roll Chai, 98
Creme Dela Oolong, 100

White Tea Blends:

Just Peachy, 104
Casablanca, 106
Pari, 108
Atoosa, 110

Herbal Teas Blends:

Serenitea, 114
Claritea, 116
Setareh (Star), 118
Cinnamon Tea, 120
Gypsy, 122
Borage Tea, 124
Majesty, 126
Mahasti Chai, 128
Pardis, 130

Black tea Blends:

as follows..

Classic Persian Tea

Black tea blend scented with Bergamot essential oil, this tea has a distinctive earthy flavor, with strong notes of honey and is the classic Persian tea blend.

Ingredients

½ cup Assam black tea
½ cup Ceylon black tea
4 droplets bergamot essential oil

Method

1. In a metal mixing bowl place Assam black tea, Ceylon black tea, and combined ingredients with a large metal mixing spoon. Next add the droplets of bergamot essential oil, and mix.

2. Next place tea in an airtight container and store at room temperature.

Persian Rose Tea

"A rose is a rose is a rose is a rose" – Gertrude Stein's seminal poem inspired this tea blend. A medley of natural rose petals and the balanced composition of black tea, make for a memorable tea experience.

Ingredients

1 cup Ceylon black tea
¼ cup rose petals

Method

1. In a mortar and pestle place rose petal into the mortar and pestle and lightly crush the petals.

2. Next transfer the petals into a metal mixing bowl. Add Ceylon black tea, and combined ingredients with a large metal mixing spoon.

3. Next place tea in an airtight container and store at room temperature.

Namaste Chai

A hand-crafted evocative blend of Assam black tea, pink peppercorns, green cardamom, star anise, ginger, and whole cloves. Invigorating and warming, Namaste Chai may be either steeped or traditionally boiled in water with milk (add a handful of chopped fresh ginger for additional heat, if desired) and sweeten with honey to taste. Fragrant and seductive, chai is perfect to enjoy anytime and makes your home smell utterly divine.

Ingredients

2/3 cup Assam Black Tea
10 green cardamom pods
7 whole star anise
2 4-inch Ceylon cinnamon sticks
1/2 tbsp. whole pink peppercorns
1/2 tbsp. whole black peppercorns
1/2 tbsp. coriander seeds
1 tbsp. allspice berries
1 tbsp. whole cloves

1 tbsp. nutmeg powder
3 tbsp. chopped candied ginger

Method:

1. Adjust oven rack to the middle position, and preheat oven to 350°F. Line one baking sheet with parchment paper.

2. With a sharp knife, split the cardamom pods in half, and place onto the prepared baking sheet along with the peppercorns, coriander, cloves, allspice berries, and cinnamon. Toast in the oven for 5 minutes, or until the spices are fragrant. Remove from oven and let cool to room temperature.

3. In a mortar and pestle place toasted spices, mix and crush.

4. Next transfer crushed ingredients into a metal mixing bowl. Add Assam black tea, nutmeg powder, chopped candied ginger, and combined ingredients with a large metal mixing spoon.

5. Next place tea in an airtight container and store at room temperature.

Grand Bazaar

Channeling the majestic splendor of the Grand Bazaar, this spice-infused delicacy inspires with each sip. This tea blend takes you on a sublime, savory tea journey throughout the bustling Grand Bazaar..

Ingredients

3/4 cup Ceylon black tea
1/4 cup rose petals
1 oz. rosehips
1/4 cup shelled pistachios
2 Pinches Saffron

Method

1. In a mortar and pestle place pistachios, and lightly crush. Then add the rose petal to the mortar and pestle and lightly crush the petals.

2. Next transfer the ingredients into a metal mixing bowl. Add Ceylon black tea, rosehips, saffron, and combined ingredients with a large metal mixing spoon.

3. Next place tea in an airtight container and store at room temperature.

Turkish Apple

This robust apple fusion - when steeped as an iced tea, transforms into a remarkably refreshing thirst-quencher. This tea is a traditionally Turkish, Azeri tea blend drunk on the Turkey, Azerbaijan, Iran border.

Ingredients

1/2 cup Assam black tea
1/2 cup Ceylon black tea
1 large green apple
1 tbsp. citric acid

Method

1. Adjust oven rack to the middle position, and preheat oven to 225°F. Line one baking sheet with parchment paper.

2. Slice apples as thinly as possible, about 1/8-inch or thinner (use a mandolin if you have one), and arrange slices onto the prepared baking sheet. Bake for 1½ hours, then flip slices and continue baking for 1 ½ hour or until completely dry and crisp. Remove from oven and let cool to room temperature.

3. In a mortar and pestle place dried apples and lightly crush.

4. Next transfer the crushed apples into a metal mixing bowl. Add Assam black tea, Ceylon black tea, citric acid, and combined ingredients with a large metal mixing spoon.

5. Next place tea in an airtight container and store at room temperature.

Cozy Monkey

This sexy aphrodisiac tea has chocolate, which contains the compounds anandamide and phenylethylamine, the first being a psychoactive feel-good chemical, and the second the "love" chemical. Both claim to induce excitement, attraction, and euphoria. As a added luxury this tea contains Capsaicin, thanks to the spicy peppers, capsaicin increases circulation and stimulates nerve endings so you'll be sure to be all hot and bothered.

Ingredients

1/2 cup Ceylon black tea
1/4 vegan chocolate chips
1 oz. whole cloves
4 tbsp. whole chili tepin
1 tbsp. cinnamon powder
1 tbsp. nutmeg powder

Method:

1. In a mortar and pestle place cloves and completely crush the pods. Then add the vegan chocolate chips and lightly crush.

2. Next transfer the ingredients into a metal mixing bowl. Add Ceylon black tea, chili tepien, cinnamon powder, nutmeg powder and combined ingredients with a large metal mixing spoon.

3. Next place tea in an airtight container and store at room temperature.

Tabriz Beauty

A comforting flavored black tea with lavender, bergamot oil, and blue mallow. Blue Mallow is used to cool both the body and mind, this herb has been known to be a wonderful throat soother, as well as having anti-inflammatory properties, reduces cholesterol levels and aids in slimming. This tea is smooth and delicious – perfect for any occasion.

Ingredients

1 cup Ceylon black tea
1 oz. dried blue mallow flower
1 oz. dried lavender
4 droplets bergamot essential oil

Method

1. In a metal mixing bowl place Ceylon black tea, dried blue mallow flower, dried lavender, and combined ingredients with a large metal mixing spoon. Next add the 4 droplets of bergamot essential oil, and mix.

2. Next place tea in an airtight container and store at room temperature.

Lover's tea

Aromatic, and sensuous. . It's the perfect brew for a cozy, romantic evening with the one you love. This tea is equally seductive over ice.

Ingredients

1 cup Ceylon black tea
1/4 cup dried rose petals
1/4 cup dried rose buds
1 oz. green cardamom pods
Pinch of saffron

Method

1. In a metal mixing bowl place Ceylon black tea, dried rose petals, dried rose buds, green cardamom pods, pinch of saffron, and combined ingredients with a large metal mixing spoon.

2. Next place tea in an airtight container and store at room temperature.

green tea Blends:

as follows..

Salam (Hello)

A refined and distinctive blend of monkey picked green tea, sencha green tea and matcha green tea. Also delicious iced.

Ingredients

1/4 cup monkey picked green tea
1/4 cup Sencha green tea
4 tbsp. matcha green tea

Method

1. In a metal mixing bowl place monkey picked green tea, Sencha green tea, matcha green tea, and combined ingredients with a large metal mixing spoon.

2. Next place tea in an airtight container and store at room temperature.

Enlighten Mint

This tea delivers delicate notes of fine cut spearmint leaves that mingle perfectly with anti-oxidant rich gunpowder green tea, creating an infusion that is as refined as it is refreshing, and thirst quenching. Drink warm or chilled. Traditionally served with fresh mint and honey.

Ingredients

1 cup gunpowder green tea
2/3 cup dried spearmint

Method

1. In a metal mixing bowl place gunpowder green tea, dried spearmint, and combined ingredients with a large metal mixing spoon.

2. Next place tea in an airtight container and store at room temperature.

Whirling Dervish

Citrusy and refreshing, this infusion steeps a mellow, light green cup. Perfect as an iced tea or as a mid-afternoon pick me up.

Ingredients

3/4 cup Sencha green tea
1 oz. dried marigold petals

Method:

1. Place Sencha green tea, dried marigolds petals into a metal mixing bowl, and combined ingredients with a large metal mixing spoon.

2. Next place tea in an airtight container and store at room temperature.

Sabzi

Sabzi meaning green in Farsi, this tea is a bend of sencha green tea flavored with lemon verbena and lemon grass. The combination of green tea makes this a perfect drink to eliminate body toxins and to reinvigorate the body throughout the day. This tea is refreshing and delicious if served iced in the summertime.

Ingredients

1/2 cup Sencha green tea
2 oz. dried lemon verbena
2 oz. dried lemongrass

Method

1. Place Sencha Green tea, dried lemon verbena, dried lemongrass into a metal mixing bowl, and combined ingredients with a large metal mixing spoon.

2. Next place tea in an airtight container and store at room temperature.

Beauty Tea

An age-old skin treatment originating from Ancient Persia, jasmine is celebrated for its toning and moisturizing properties. Combining jasmine celebrated healing properties with ginseng: which detoxes the skin, fights premature aging, and aids in weight loss. This tea is the ultimate beauty beverage.

Ingredients

½ cup jasmine pearl green tea
12 thin slices of fine dried ginseng root
1 oz. dried jasmine buds

Method

1. Place Jasmine pearl green tea, sliced dried ginseng root, dried jasmine buds into a metal mixing bowl, and combined ingredients with a large metal mixing spoon.

2. Next place tea in an airtight container and store at room temperature.

Aroosi

Celebrate long-lasting affection and potent lust with this luxurious tea. According to Ayurvedic medicine, the lotus flower represents eternity, purity, and divinity, and In Persian culture the lotus flower symbolizes beauty, sensuality and sexuality. So this is the perfect tea for your Aroosi (wedding/ wedding party).

Ingredients:

1/2 cup jasmine pearl green tea
5 dried whole lotus flower
5 dried shirazi figs, sliced in half
1 oz. dried Jasmine buds

Method:

1. Place jasmine pearl green tea, dried lotus flowers, shirazi figs, dried jasmine buds into a metal mixing bowl, and combined ingredients with a large metal mixing spoon.

2. Next place tea in an airtight container and store at room temperature.

Magnificent

Sencha green tea layered with rose petals. This delicate green tea is a delight with delicious floral notes and an unmistakable floral bouquet. This blend is turly magnificent.

Ingredients

3/4 cup Sencha green tea
1 oz. dried rose petals

Method

1. Place Sencha green tea, dried rose petals into a metal mixing bowl, and combined ingredients with a large metal mixing spoon.

2. Next place tea in an airtight container and store at room temperature.

Oolong tea Blends:

as follows..

Rumi Tea

Oolong is loved for it's complex and refined taste as well as it's ability to reduce cholesterol and aids in weight loss - blended with dainty chrysanthemum flowers know to cleanse the body as a whole, this tea blend dazzles with a savory aroma, rich body and smooth delicate flavor – the perfect tea for a spa day.

Ingredients:

1/2 cup fine oolong tea
2 oz. cup dried chrysanthemum

Method:

1. Place fine oolong tea, chrysanthemum into a metal mixing bowl, and combined ingredients with a large metal mixing spoon.

2. Next place tea in an airtight container and store at room temperature.

Imperial Label

Start your day with an uplifting cup of this robust and flavorful infusion. Perfect for a seamless transition into the world of tea, this bold infusion offers the best of both worlds. Bee pollen is one of nature's secret gems! It has an amazing source of protein that is both easily-digested and assimilated by the body. It is also high in antioxidants lycopene, selenium, and beta-carotene, which help protect the body from disease.

Ingredients

1/2 cup fine grade oolong tea
1 oz. cup bee pollen

Method

1. Place fine grade oolong tea, bee pollen into a metal mixing bowl, and combined ingredients with a large metal mixing spoon.

2. Next place tea in an airtight container and store at room temperature.

Rock & Roll Chai

Nothing can quite compare to the sheer energy of Rock & Roll. But I've tried to capture the essence with this lively, colorful chai. It's a delicately sweet oolong tea blend with all - the warm, comforting flavors of a fresh spice cake... Not to mention the fun, vibrant pop of pink peppercorns, and tangerines. It'll have you singing and dancing to your favorite song in no time.

Ingredients

1/2 cup fine grade oolong tea
1 tangerine
5 green cardamom pods
2 4-inch Ceylon cinnamon sticks
2 tbsp. whole pink peppercorns
2 tbsp. whole cloves
2 tbsp. ginger powder

Method

1. Adjust oven rack to the middle position, and preheat oven to 200°F. Line one baking sheet with parchment paper.

2. Slice the tangerine fruit as thinly as possible, about 1/8-inch or thinner (use a mandolin if you have one), and arrange slices onto the prepared baking sheet. Bake for 1½ hours, then flip slices and continue baking for 1 ½ hour or until completely dry. Remove from oven and let cool to room temperature.

3. In a mortar and pestle place cardamom pods, cinnamon sticks and crush ingredients.

4. Place crushed ingredients, tangerine slices, orchid oolong tea, pink peppercorns, whole cloves, ginger powder into a metal mixing bowl, and combined ingredients with a large metal mixing spoon.

5. Next place tea in an airtight container and store at room temperature.

Crème de la Oolong

Immerse yourself into a cup of this dreamy infusion! With its light body and smooth creamy texture, it's the crème de la crème! This blend delivers a sweet and soothing balance of vanilla, almond, and its great warm, or as a dessert tea.

Ingredients:

1/2 cup fine grade oolong tea
1 oz. organic almond milk powder
1 vanilla bean (split lengthwise, scraped, & let pods and seeds dry overnight)

Method:

1. Place oolong tea, organic almond milk powder, vanilla pod and seeds into a metal mixing bowl, and combined ingredients with a large metal mixing spoon.

2. Next place tea in an airtight container and store at room temperature.

White tea Blends:

as follows..

Just Peachy

Delightful and refreshing, this wonderfully distinctive tea exhibits light flavor of ripened peaches. This tea creates a wonderfully light and refreshing infusion.

Ingredients

1/2 cup high grade white tea
1 peach

Method

1. Adjust oven rack to the middle position, and preheat oven to 200°F. Line one baking sheet with parchment paper.

2. Slice the peach fruit as thinly as possible, about 1/8-inch or thinner (use a mandolin if you have one), and arrange slices onto the prepared baking sheet. Bake for 1½ hours, then flip slices and continue baking for 1½ hours or until completely dry. Remove from oven and let cool to room temperature.

3. Place high grade white tea, and dried peach slices into a metal mixing bowl, and combined ingredients with a large metal mixing spoon.

4. Next place tea in an airtight container and store at room temperature.

Casablanca

Jasmine is widely known to lower blood pressure, strengthen the immune system, lower cholesterol levels and regulate aging processes in our bodies. While the lovely fragrance of jasmine is known to have a calming effect that soothe the nerves, and liquor is refreshing and has a cooling effect on the body. The exotic fragrances of jasmine will transport you to the time of 1001 nights.

Ingredients:

1/2 cup white sliver needle tea
1 oz. dried Jasmine Buds

Method:

1. Place silver needle white tea, and dried Jasmine Buds into a metal mixing bowl, and combined ingredients with a large metal mixing spoon.

2. Next place tea in an airtight container and store at room temperature.

Experience the many wonders of quince in this uplifting white tea blend, with its refreshing floral notes and its smooth, rounded finish. Traditionally Zoroastrians (an ancient Iranian religion / a religious philosophy) considered the quince a symbol of love, happiness and fertility. Still to this day many Persians eat quince at wedding feasts, and the new bride will take a bite of a quince to add fragrance to her wedding night kisses.

Ingredients

1/2 cup high grade white tea
1 oz. dried marigold petals
1 quince

Method

1. Adjust oven rack to the middle position, and preheat oven to 200°F. Line one baking sheet with parchment paper.

2. Slice the quince fruit as thinly as possible, about 1/8-inch or thinner (use a mandolin if you have one), and arrange slices onto the prepared baking sheet. Bake for 1½ hours, then flip slices and continue baking for 1½ hours or until completely dry. Remove from oven and let cool to room temperature.

3. Place high grade white tea, dried marigold petals, and dried quince slices into a metal mixing bowl, and combined ingredients with a large metal mixing spoon.

4. Next place tea in an airtight container and store at room temperature.

atoosa

Love thy self with this detox tea. The combination of white tea, goji berries, and chia seeds makes atoosa the perfect drink to detoxify and reinvigorate the body. This cleanse will assist with reducing weight, easing bloating, increasing digestion functionality, improves skin clarity, increasing energy levels and alleviate issues associated with food intolerances. Formulated with ayurvedic principles.

Ingredients

1/2 cup white sliver needle tea
2 oz. goji berries
1 oz. chia seed powder

Method

1. Place silver needle white tea, goji berries,and chia seed powder into a metal mixing bowl, and combined ingredients with a large metal mixing spoon.

2. Next place tea in an airtight container and store at room temperature.

Herbal tea Blends:

as follows..

Serenitea

A soothing blend of chrysanthemum, spearmint, and chamomile yields a sunny bouquet. This herbal tea is the perfect nightcap that will send you off to a blissful sleep.

Ingredients

1/2 cup dried white chrysanthemum
1/4 cup dried spearmint
2 oz. dried chamomile flowers

Method

1. Place dried white chrysanthemum, dried spearmint, dried chamomile flowers into a metal mixing bowl, and combined ingredients with a large metal mixing spoon.

2. Next place tea in an airtight container and store at room temperature.

Claritea

This citrus blend of purifying herbs combines delicious flavor, and is a gentle, yet effective way of regulating the body's natural cleansing process. This Ayurvedic inspired tea blend is crafted to enhance clarity and balance from the inside out.

1/2 cup dried lemon verbena
2 oz. lemon Balm
1 lemon
1 pink grapefruit

1. Adjust oven rack to the middle position, and preheat oven to 200°F. Line one baking sheet with parchment paper.

2. Slice the lemon, and pink grapefruit as thinly as possible, about 1/8-inch or thinner (use a mandolin if you have one), and arrange slices onto the prepared baking sheet. Bake for 1½ hours, then flip slices and continue baking for 1½ hours or until completely dry. Remove from oven and let cool to room temperature.

3. In a metal mixing bowl place dried lemon slices, dried grapefruit slices, dried lemon verbena, dried lemon balm, and combined ingredients with a large metal mixing spoon.

4. Next place tea in an airtight container and store at room temperature.

Setareh (star)

This tea is caffeine free, rich in antioxidants and calcium, mulberry-leaf tea produces a rich, fruity and sweet brew. While yielding a unusually rich and delightful flavor. This tea helps to support healthy blood pressure and cholesterol levels, a healthy digestive system, and assists in weight management.

Ingredients:

1/2 cup mulberry leaf
2 oz. dried rose hips

Method:

1. Place dried mulberry leaf, dried rose hips into a metal mixing bowl, and combined ingredients with a large metal mixing spoon.

2. Next place tea in an airtight container and store at room temperature.

Cinnamon Tea

A soothing elixir, this simple tisane has a remarkable effect in rejuvenating both body and mind thanks to antioxidants called polyphenols, which help boost the immune system and fight damaging free radicals.

Ingredients

7 cinnamon sticks

Method

1. In a mortar and pestle place cinnamon sticks and crush.

2. Next place tea in an airtight container and store at room temperature.

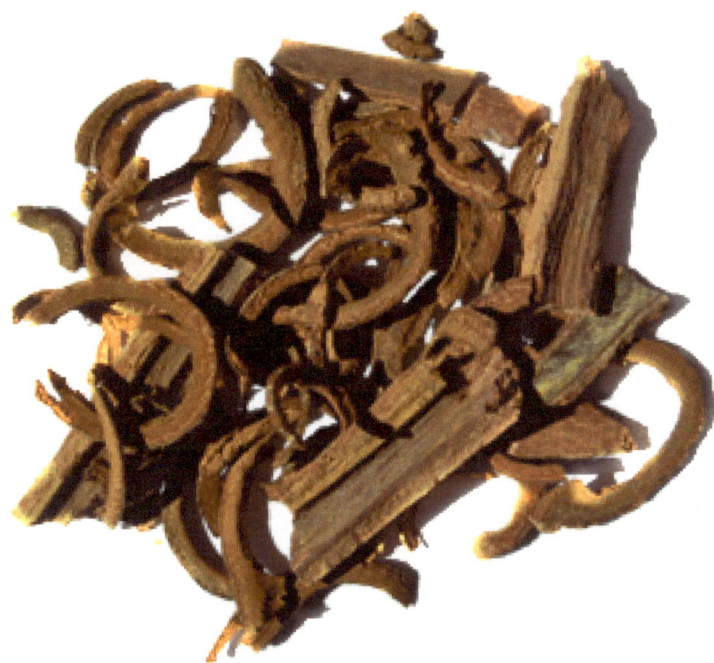

Gypsy

This ravishing scarlet-hued brew, pleasantly tart and high in vitamin C, and is equally delicious hot or over ice. Allegedly, Cleopatra adored hibiscus tea and believed it enhanced her legendary beauty.

Ingredients:

1 cup dried hibiscus flower
2 oz. dried cherries
1 oz. dried rose petals
1 orange

Method:

1. Adjust oven rack to the middle position, and preheat oven to 200°F. Line one baking sheet with parchment paper.

2. Slice the orange as thinly as possible, about 1/8-inch or thinner (use a mandolin if you have one), and arrange slices onto the prepared baking sheet. Bake for 1½ hours, then flip slices and continue baking for 1½ hours or until completely dry. Remove from oven and let cool to room temperature.

3. In a metal mixing bowl place dried orange peels, dried hibiscus flowers, dried cherries, dried rose petals, and combined ingredients with a large metal mixing spoon.

4. Next place tea in an airtight container and store at room temperature.

Borage Tea

Borage tea in Farsi "Chai Gol Gavzaban" is a flowering plant that grows in the northern part of Iran. The name literally means "cow's tongue flower" and is know for having a calming effect on the nervous system. Readily use this herbal tea to relive stress, and help cure the common cold.

Ingredients:

1/2 cup dried borage leaf
1/4 cup dried borage flower

Method:

1. In a mortar and pestle place borage leaf, borage flower and lightly crush.

2. Next place tea in an airtight container and store at room temperature.

Majesty

From the South African red bush tree, Rooibos is naturally caffeine free and rich in antioxidants and minerals. This tea is blended with hibiscus, rose petals, rose hips, soothing lavender and black currants for a slightly exotic twist. Enjoy with friends, and as spring progresses into summer, you'll find that it's a refreshingly different iced tea.

Ingredients

1/2 cup red rooibos
2 oz. dried hibiscus flower
1 oz. dried rose petals
1 oz. dried rose hips
1 oz. dried lavender
1 oz. black currants (crushed)

Method

1. In a metal mixing bowl place red rooibos, dried hibiscus flower, dried rose petals, rose hips, dried lavender, black currants, and combined ingredients with a large metal mixing spoon.

2. Next place tea in an airtight container and store at room temperature.

Mahasti Chai

If you're into spice-based chais, this one is for you. It has a smooth base of caffeine-free rooibos, and a satisfying kick of cinnamon, cardamom and pink peppercorns. So exotic, so inviting, so warming - try it straight up or infused with hot almond milk for a truly fabulous chai latte. It's the kind of thing you get addicted to.

Ingredients

1/2 cup red rooibos
1 oz. dried marigold petals
7 green cardamom pods
7 whole star anise
4 4-inch Ceylon cinnamon sticks
2 tbsp. whole pink peppercorns
3 tbsp. whole cloves
1 tbsp. nutmeg ground

Method:

1. In a mortar and pestle place cardamom pods, cinnamon sticks and crush ingredients.

2. Next transfer crushed ingredients into a metal mixing bowl. Add marigold petals, star anise, pink peppercorns, red rooibos, cloves, and combined ingredients with a large metal mixing spoon.

3. Next place tea in an airtight container and store at room temperature.

Pardis

A sensuous tea. Unexpected flavor profile a - remarkably uncommon sensory experience. Rooibos, peppermint, and chocolate melt away into a lush brew. Not for the faint of heart, a glorious sip to tantalize your tastebuds.

Ingredients:

1/2 cup red rooibos
4 tbsp. vegan semisweet chocolate chips (crushed)
4 tbsp. dried peppermint

Method:

1. Place rooibos, chocolate chips, dried peppermint, into a metal mixing bowl, and combined ingredients with a large metal mixing spoon.

2. Next place tea in an airtight container and store at room temperature.

Chapter 7:
Hot & Cold
Beverages

Hot & Cold Beverages :

(Noshabeh)

Persian Coffee (Qahveh), 136

Spiced, Dried Fruit Punch (Ab'e Miveh), 137

Rosewater Elixir (Sharbat'e Golab), 138

Mint, Lime, Spritzer (Sharbat'e Limoo), 140

Sour Cherry Elixir (Sharbat'e Albaloo), 142

Cider Vinegar, Mint Tonic (Sharbat'e Sekanjabin), 144

Persian Cure All (Araq'e Tokhme Sharbati), 146

Persian Detox Elixir (Araq'e Khakshir), 148

Rose Milk (Shir Golab), 150

Date Milkshake (Majoon), 152

Persian Coffee
(Qahveh)

This strong coffee much like espresso is prepared in an Ibriq: a copper, or brass coffee pot with a long handle, and then poured into small porcelain cups.

Ingredients:

Fine ground Turkish coffee
Raw organic honey
Pinch of ground cardamom
Pinch of saffron
Cold Water
Small cups
A Ibriq (see note below)
Demitasse cups (small Cups)

Method:

1. Start with very cold water. Use The demitasse cup to measure the water needed for each cup of coffee (one demitasse cup of water is about 4 ounces), and pour the water into the Ibriq.

2. For each demitasse cup, add 1 teaspoon of coffee, along with 1 teaspoon of honey, pinch of ground cardamom, and a pinch of saffron.

4. Place the Ibriq on the stove top, mix ingredients together with a small wood spoon, and bring to a boil until the coffee starts to rise over high heat. Immediately remove ibrik from heat before it boils over.

5. Pour Coffee in the demitasse cup.

Note: Ibriq is a long-handled small pot usually made from copper. They are available for purchase at most Persian or Middle Eastern Markets.

Spiced, Dried Fruit Punch

(Ab'e Miveh)

For parties or any type of winter seasonal entertaining, I like to make this belly-warming comfy fruit punch, this is the perfect drink for Shab'e Yalda (the longest night of the year). This delicious punch will transport you to the fairy tales of one thousand and one nights, while filling your home with a warming allspice fragrance.

Ingredients:

2 cups alkaline water
1 cup pure pomegranate juice
1 cup freshly squeezed orange juice
(keep orange rinds)
1 vanilla pod, split down the middle to
show the seeds
2 cinnamon sticks
6 cloves
4 cardamom pods
6 whole star anise

6 quarter inch slices of fresh ginger
1 large quince, cored, cut into 1/4 inch
thick wedges
1/4 cup prunes, pitted
1/4 cup medjool dates, pitted
1/4 cup dried apricots
2 oz. dried sour cherries, pitted
1/2 cup raw organic honey
Pinch of saffron

Method:

1. In a 6-quart saucepan place pomegranate juice, water, orange juice, orange rinds, vanilla pod, cinnamon sticks, cardamom pods, star anise, quince wedges, fresh ginger, prunes, medjoon dates, dried apricots, and dried sour cherries. Cover saucepan, and simmer for 1 hour over low heat. Stir occasionally with a wooden spoon.

2. Add honey, stir until honey is completely combined. Next stir in saffron, and simmer for 5 minutes uncovered.

3. Serve warm. Ladle punch directly into serving glasses, making sure to include a few pieces of fruit for each glass.

Rosewater Elixir
(Sharbat'e Golab)

This drink is traditionally served cold at Persian weddings, and served warm after a fast.

Makes 1 bottle of syrup

Ingredients

2 cups alkaline water
1 ½ cup raw organic honey
1/2 cup rose water
1/4 cup fresh lime juice
1/4 cup rosebuds (Wrapped in a bouquet garni)

Mixing:
Plain filter water, sparkling water, or club soda
5 Ice cubes per person

Method

1. In a 4-quart porcelain or enamel saucepan place water and honey mix ingredients together until honey is completely combined. Bring to a boil, and let simmer for 10 minutes. Stir occasionally with a wooden spoon.

2. Add the lime juice, rose water, rose buds sachet, and cook, uncovered, over medium/low heat for 10 minutes or until a light rose-infused syrup has formed.

3. Remove from heat, set aside to cool. Once cooled use a slotted spoon to remove rose bud sachet from saucepan. Pour the syrup into a clean bottle and cork tightly. Store at room temperature until ready to use.

4. To serve cold, mix in a ratio of: 1 part syrup, 3 parts water (or clubs soda), and 5 ice cubes per person. Server Chilled, and garnish with mint leaves and/ or rose buds.

5. To serve warm, mix in a ratio of: 1 part syrup, 3 parts warm water.

Mint, Lime, Spritzer
Sharbat'e Limoo

This is a refreshing, sweet and sour thirst-quenching drink much like lemonade. Sharbat'e limoo is one of the most popular sharbats in Iran. This drink is traditionally made with fresh lime juice, but it can be easily substituted for fresh lemon juice.

Makes 1 bottle of syrup

Ingredients

2 cups alkaline water
1½ cup raw organic honey
1½ cup fresh lime juice, or lemon juice
Zest of one lime, or half a lemon

Mixing:
Plain filter water, sparkling water, or club soda
5 Ice cubes per person

Method:

1. In a 4-quart porcelain or enamel saucepan place water and honey mix ingredients together until honey is completely combined. Bring to a boil, and let simmer for 10 minutes. Stir occasionally with a wooden spoon.

2. Add the lime juice, lime zest, and cook, uncovered, over medium/low heat for 10 minutes or until light - lime-infused syrup has formed.

3. Remove from heat, set aside to cool. Once cooled use a slotted spoon to remove lime zest from saucepan. Pour the syrup into a clean bottle and cork tightly. Store at room temperature until ready to use.

4. To serve, mix in a ratio of: 1 part syrup, 3 parts water (or sparkling water), and 5 ice cubes per person. Server Chilled, and garnish with lime slices and/or a spring of fresh mint.

Sour Cherry Elixir

Sharbat'e Albaloo

This blush sweet and sour drink is amazing in the summertime, when I'm making this elixir I often use sparkling water, for a refreshing sparkling beverage, and garnish with a cherry on top!

Makes 1 bottle of syrup

Ingredients:

2 Cups alkaline water
1 ½ cup organic raw honey
1/4 cup fresh lime juice
1 pound fresh sour cherries (wrapped in a bouquet garni)
¼ tbsp. pure vanilla extract

Mixing:
Plain filter water, sparkling water, or club soda
5 Ice cubes per person

Method:

1. In a 4-quart porcelain or enamel saucepan place water and honey, mix ingredients together until honey is completely combined. Bring to a boil, and let simmer for 10 minutes. Stir occasionally with a wooden spoon.

2. Add the lime juice, cherry sachet, and cook, uncovered, over medium/low heat for 20 minutes or until light - cherry-infused syrup has formed.

3. Remove from heat, add vanilla extract, and set aside to cool. Once cooled, remove cherry sachet from saucepan. Pour the syrup into a clean bottle and cork tightly. Keep refrigerated, and use as needed.

4. To serve, mix in a ratio of: 1 part syrup, 3 parts water (or sparkling water), and 5 ice cubes per person. Server Chilled, and garnish with a fresh cherry.

Cider Vinegar, Mint Tonic
(Sharbat'e Sekanjabin)

This medieval drink was known by the ancient Greeks as oxymel, and was a favorite of the legendary shahs (kings) of Iran's past. This syrup can be served as a beverage, or served as a dip alongside crisp Romaine leaves.

Makes 1 bottle of syrup

Ingredients

2 cups alkaline water
1 ½ cup raw organic honey
1/2 cup apple cider vinegar
1 bunch fresh mint, washed, drained, and wrapped in a bouquet garni

Mixing:
Plain filter water, sparkling water, or club soda
5 Ice cubes per person

Garnish:
1/4 cup finely shredded cucumber
2 tbsp. finely chopped mint

Method

1. In a 4-quart porcelain or enamel saucepan place water and honey mix ingredients together until honey is completely combined. Bring to a boil, and let simmer for 10 minutes. Stir occasionally with a wooden spoon.

2. Add the vinegar, mint sachet, and cook, uncovered over medium/ low heat for 20 minutes or until light, mint-infused syrup has formed.

3. Remove from heat, and set aside to cool. Once cooled, remove mint sachet from saucepan. Pour the syrup into a clean bottle and cork tightly. Store at room temperature until ready to use.

4. To serve, mix in a ratio of: 1 part syrup, 3 parts water (or sparkling water), and 5 ice cubes per person. Server chilled, garnish with shredded cucumber, and mint leaves.

Persian Cure All Elixir
(Araq'e Tokhme Sharbati)

This is a treasured family secret know as a cure all elixir that is packed with omega 3's thanks to the chia seeds. I drink this four times a week as it aids in overall good health - along with weight management, and mental clarity.

Serves 4

Ingredients

2½ cups alkaline water
1/2 cup fresh lemon or lime juice
1/4 cup raw organic honey
1/2 bunch fresh mint, finely chopped
2 oz. rosewater
2 tbsp. chia seeds (Tokhme Sharbati)

Garnish:
a spring of mint.

Method

1. Place all ingredients in a large pitcher, and with a spoon mix all ingredients together. Refrigerate for at least 2 hours before serving.

2. Serve with ice cubes, and garnish with a spring of mint.

Persian detox

(Araq'e Khakshir)

This ancient Persian detox has been passed down through generations in my family. This drink features the natural detoxifying powers of rose water, and healing properties of beta-carotene from the cantaloupe, combined with teff seed – which contains all 8 essential amino acids. This delicious elixir boosting with antibacterial and anti-inflammatory properties, will bring balance to your diet. Serves 2

Ingredients

2 cup cantaloupe juice (freshly pressed)
½ cup rose water
1 tbsp. teff seeds (Khakshir)

Garnish:
a organic rose.

Method:

1. Place all ingredients in a large pitcher, and with a spoon mix all ingredients together. Refrigerate for at least 2 hours before serving.

2. Serve with ice cubes, and garnish with a organic rose.

Rose Milk
(Shir Golab)

My mother would make this aromatic comforting bedtime drink for me every night as a child to ensure that I would have a wholesome sleep. This is an ancient Sufi remedy that is said to be created by Rumi.

Serves 2

Ingredients

1 cup almond milk
2 tbsp rose water
3 tbsp. raw organic honey
pinch of saffron

Garnish:
pinch of saffron

Method

1. In a medium saucepan place almond milk and gently warm milk over low heat. Add rose water and honey, and stir until honey is completely combined. Next stir in saffron, and simmer for 2 minutes uncovered.

2. Pour mixture into serving glasses, and garnish with threads of saffron.

Date Milkshake

(Majoon)

This elegant shake is simply majestic, and is bursting with flavor. This shake was customarily only consumed by men, as it was considered an aphrodisiac that would aid in the process of producing a male heir. I know this sounds quite silly - with that being said my grandmother full-heartedly believes this old wives tale.

Serves 2

Ingredients

1 cup cold almond milk
2 bananas
2 scoops of thick yogurt
5 majdoul dates (pits removed)
2 tbsp. crushed pistachios
1 tbsp. yellow raisins
½ cup ice

Garnish:
1 tbsp. crushed rose petals (optional)
1 tbsp. crushed pistachios (optional)
1 tbsp. shaved coconut (optional)

Method

1. In a blender place: almond milk, bananas, thick yogurt, majdoul dates, crushed pistachios, raisins, ice, and blend all ingredients together until smooth.

2. Pour mixture into serving glasses, and garnish with rose petals, crushed pistachios, and shaved coconut.

Chapter 8: Tea Luxurious

Rice Cookies (Nan'e Berenji), 158

Saffron Pistachio Toffee (Sohan'e Qum), 159

Dainty Sugared Almonds (Noghl), 160

Dense Rose Water Confection (Halva), 162

Persian Baklava (Baghlava), 164

Star Cake (Cake'e Setareh), 166

Quince Preserves (Moraba'ye Beh), 168

Sour Cherry Preserves (Moraba'ye Albalu), 169

Rose Petal Preserves (Moraba'ye Gol'e Sorkh), 170

Savory:

(Mezze)

Persian Trail Mix (Ajil), 172

Pomegranate Marinated Olives (Zeytoon Parvardeh), 174

Stuffed dates (Mezze'e Khorma), 175

Stuffed Grape Leaves (Dolmeh), 176

Barbari Bread (Nan'e Barbari), 178

Aromatic Herb Starter (Sabzi Khordan), 180

Yogurt & Cucumber Starter (Mast'o Khiar), 182

Farmer's Cheese (Panir), 184

Mamani's Spicy Feta Dip (Panir Mamani), 186

Tomato & Cucumber Salad (Salad'e Shirazi), 188

Watermelon, Rose Water Salad (Salad'e Hendevaneh va Panir), 190

Rice cookies
(Nan'e Berenji)

These luxe little white cookies sprinkled with poppy seeds simply "melt in your mouth", and pair wonderfully with a warm cup of tea.

Makes 25 Cookies

Ingredients

1 cup melted ghee (roghan'e kareh)
1 cup confectioners' sugar
2 eggs
3 cups fine rice flour, sifted
4 tbsp rose water
2 tbsp. ground cardamom

Garnish:
1 tbsp. poppy seeds

Method

1. Using a stand mixer fitted with a flat paddle attachment, cream ghee and sugar together for 4 minutes. Add eggs, rose water, and ground cardamom and combine.

2. Add the rice flour one cup at a time, gently mixing until the dough is evenly incorporated (making sure not to over-mix the mixture).

3. Form the dough into a ball, wrap with plastic wrap, and refrigerate overnight.

4. Adjust oven rack to the middle position, and preheat oven to 350° F.
Line a Baking sheet with parchment paper, or a non-stick baking mat.

5. Using a small ice cream scoop, roll dough into small balls, place cookies ½-inch apart on the prepared baking sheet.

6. Lightly flatten dough balls using the back of a spoon. Next use the side on the spoon to lightly press a design on the top of each cookie, and sprinkle each cookie with poppy seeds.

7. Place baking sheet in the oven and bake for 15-20 minutes, or until the color changes slightly. Remove the baking sheet from oven. Place the baking sheet on a cooling rack, and let cool thoroughly. When removing cookies from the tray handle with care, these cookies are quite delicate, and tend to crumble very easily.

Saffron Pistachio Toffee
(Sohan'e Qom)

This is the most famous Persian toffee recipe from the holy city Qom. Qum is renowned for its shrines, and is considered by Shia Muslims to be the second most sacred city in Iran after Mashhad. This candy is seldom made at home, because whenever someone pilgrims to Qom, they return with copious amounts of toffee to share with their family and friends.

Make about 15 toffee

Ingredients:

1 cup granulated sugar
1/4 cup ghee (roghan'e kareh)
1/2 tsp. ground saffron
2 tsp. ground cardamom
1/4 cup slivered pistachios

Garnish:
¼ cup crushed pistachios
2 tsp. crushed rose petals

Method:

1. Line one baking sheet with parchment paper. Set aside.

2. In a medium-saucepan place sugar, ghee, and combine over a medium heat, while stirring constantly with a wooden spoon until the sugar has dissolved (about 5 minutes). Increase the heat to high and cook until the mixture begins to become golden in color. Add saffron, cardamom, slivered pistachios and stir. Continue to cook for 5 minutes until the mixture is golden brown.

3. Remove from heat immediately, and quickly spoon mixture (forming small circles about 2-inchs in diameter) onto prepared baking sheets. Sprinkle each toffee with crushed pistachios, and crushed rose petals.

4. Allow the toffee to cool at room temperature for 1 hour. Once cooled remove toffee from the parchment paper using an offset spatula. Store in an airtight container.

Dainty Sugared Almonds

Noghl, are dainty whimsical candies made from sugar and almonds. Noghl are served at all Persian weddings, and given away as wedding favors to represent love and fertility for the newlyweds. These candies are also served with warm tea and used like sugar cubes.

Ingredients

1 cup baking sugar
1/2 cup rosewater
1 cup blanched silvered almonds

Method

1. Line one baking sheet with parchment paper. Set aside.

2. In a medium-saucepan place sugar, rosewater, and bring to a boil over medium-high heat for 15 minutes, or cook until 266° F. registers on a candy thermometer.

3. In a separate saucepan place ½ cup of almonds, and carefully add half of the hot syrup to the almonds, while constantly shaking and tossing the almonds until fully coated. Place coated almonds onto prepared baking sheet, and let cool. Repeat process for remaining almonds.

4. Once cooled separate coated almonds, and store in an airtight container.

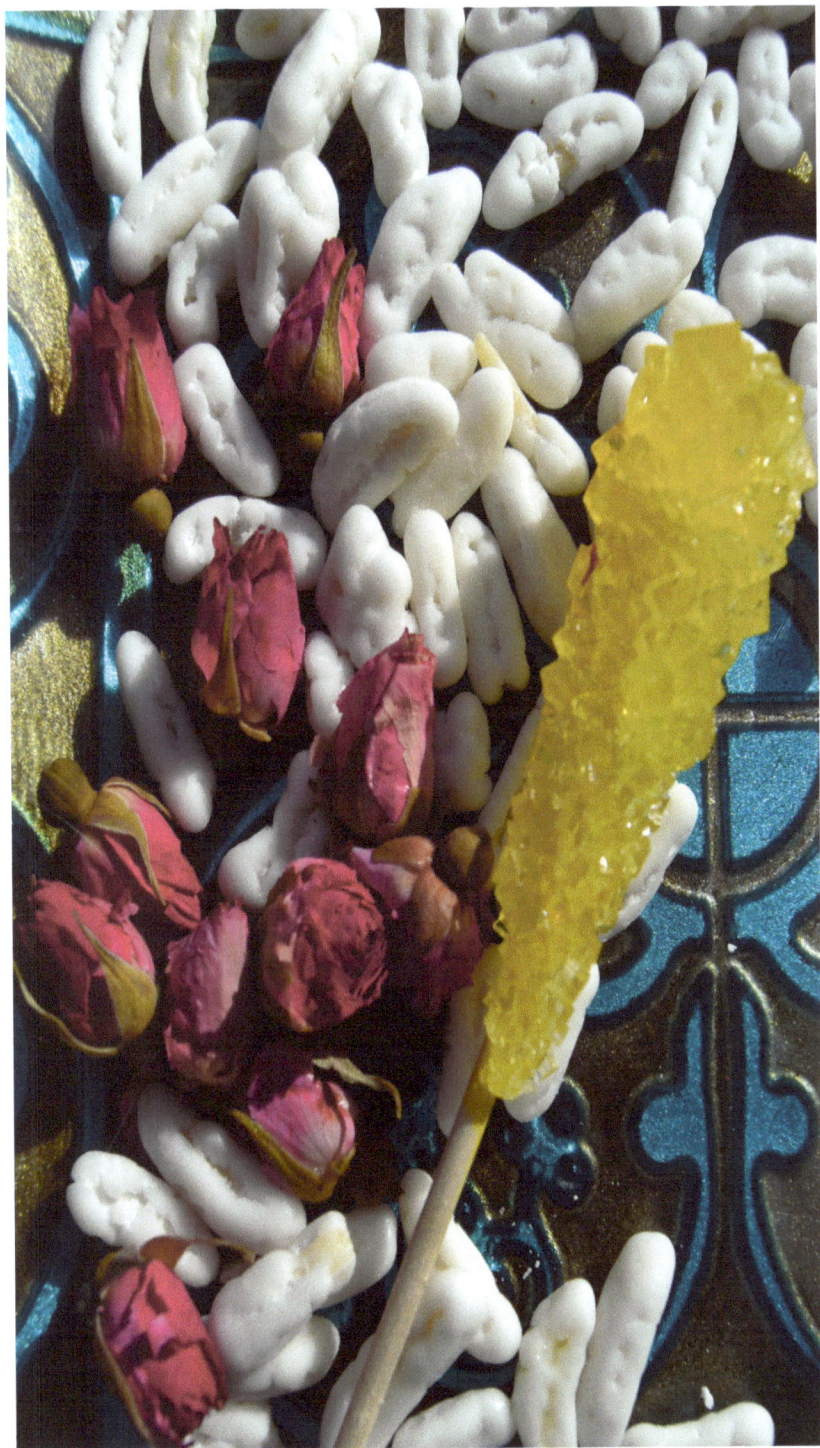

Dense Rose Water Confection
(Halva)

Persian Halva is a sweet honey-flavored dessert made from flour, and is an ancient recipe that date back to the 18th century. Halva is traditional served during the month of Ramadan, and is eaten during the fast-breaking meal know as Eftar with warm tea

Ingredients

1 cup all-purpose flour, sifted
1 cup water
2/3 cup granulated sugar
1 cup ghee (roghan'e kareh)
1/2 cup rose water
Pinch of saffron threads (grinded & dissolved in 2 tbsp. hot water)

Garnish:
¼ cup crushed pistachios
2 tsp. crushed rose petals

Method

1. In a medium-saucepan place sugar, water, and bring to a boil over medium heat, stir constantly with a wooden spoon until the sugar has dissolved (about 5 minutes). Let simmer for 5 more minutes, or until a thin syrup forms. Remove from heat. Add saffron liquid, rose water and combined. Set aside.

2. In another medium-sized saucepan, place flour and toast over high heat while string constantly, until golden in color (no longer than 2 minutes). Reduce heat to medium, add ghee and cook for 7-10 minutes, still stirring constantly, until mixture forms into a smooth paste. Remove from heat.

4. Carefully add the syrup to the flour mixture, and mix vigorously for one minute, or until smooth. Then return the saucepan to the stove, over low heat, stirring continually until all the syrup has been absorbed into the mixture, and a smooth paste forms (approximately 4 minutes).

5. Remove from heat, and transfer halva to a serving plate, smooth and flatten the surface with the back of a spoon, and imprint half-moons into the surface using the side of a spoon. Or spread the halva onto a cleaned flat surface, and cut into shapes using a small cookie cutter. Garnish with crushed pistachios, and crushed rose petals. Refrigerate until well chilled.

Persian Baklava
(Baghlava)

Baklava is a traditional treat throughout the Mediterranean. Persian baklava is traditionally made with a thick tart like dough, however my recipe uses ready-made Phyllo-dough. The end result makes a buttery, nut-filled pastry soaked in a honey rose water infused syrup.

Ingredients

14 sheets Phyllo dough (1 packet)
1/2 cup ghee (melted)

For the syrup:
1 cup raw organic honey
1 cup water
1/2 cup rose water
1/2 cup granulated sugar
Pinch of saffron threads, grounded
1 tbsp. cinnamon

For the filling:
3 cup slivered pistachios, or almonds
1/2 cup granulated sugar
1 tbsp. ground cardamom
1 tbsp. ground cinnamon

Garnish:
¼ cup crushed pistachios

Method

1. Adjust oven rack to the middle position, and preheat oven to 350° F.

2. In a Medium-saucepan place honey, water, sugar, ground cinnamon and bring to a boil over medium heat, stir constantly with a wooden spoon until the sugar has dissolved (about 5 minutes). Let simmer for 5 more minutes, or until a thin syrup forms. Remove from heat. Add saffron liquid, rose water and combined. Set aside.

3. Prepare the filling by placing slivered pistachios, sugar, ground cardamom, and ground cinnamon into a food processor. Pulse until finely ground.

4. Brush a baking sheet (14 x 10 inches) with melted ghee, and lay down 7 sheets of filo pastry, brushing between each layer with melted ghee, spread the nut mixture over the filo pastry, and evenly press it down. Top with remaining 7 filo sheets, brushing between each layer with melted butter.

5. Using a sharp knife, carefully cut the baklava into 12 diamonds.

6. Bake for 35-45 minutes until golden. Remove from oven, and evenly pour the cold syrup over the hot baklava. Garnish with crushed pistachios. Leave to cool at room temperature, for at least 8 hours.

Note: Baklava is best enjoyed at room temperature, do not refrigerate.

164

Star Cake

(Cake'e Setareh

This is one of my favorite cakes. It's moist and dense, and filled with aromatic edible roses. Its truly delicious and supper impressive-looking; thanks to the fresh roses adorned at the top and bottom of the cake. The Farsi name for this cake is "Setareh" which means star, and this cake is a ture star.

Ingredients

2 cups cake flower, (not self-rising)
2 tsp. baking powder
1/8 tsp. salt
1 cup unsalted butter, softened
1 cup full-fat plain yogurt
1 tsp. pure vanilla extract
1 ½ cup granulated sugar, sifted
6 egg whites (at room temperature)
1/4 cup fresh edible rose petals, diced, loosely-packed

Frosting:
12 oz cream cheese (room temperature)
1½ cups heavy cream
1 cup confectioners' sugar, sifted
2 tbsp. rose water

Garnish:
1 cup fresh edible roses

Method

1. To prepare the filling: in a medium mixing bowl place heavy cream, and whisk until medium to stiff peaks form (about 5 minutes). Set aside. In a separate mixing bowl place cream cheese, confectioners' sugar, rose water, and whip until smooth. Using a rubber spatula, Gradually fold the whipped cream into the cream cheese mixture. Set aside, and refrigerate until ready to use.

2. Adjust oven rack to the middle position, and preheat oven to 350° F.
Line 3 6x2-inch round cake pans with parchment paper rounds, and butter pans.

3. In a medium bowl sift flour, baking powder, and salt together. Set aside. In the bowl of an stand mixer fitted with a paddle attachment, place butter, 1 cup sugar and mix together until light and fluffy, about 4 minutes. Add vanilla, place mixer on low, and gradually add flour mixture, alternating by adding yogurt, and continue beating until the batter is evenly incorporated (making sure not to over-mix the batter). Add ¼ cup rose petals, and combine. Transfer batter to a large bowl, and set aside.

4. In the clean bowl of a stand mixer fitted with a whisk attachment, place egg whites, and beat on low speed until foamy. Next gradually add remaining 1/2 cup sugar, and beat on high speed until stiff, glossy peaks form (making sure not to over-beat the mixture). Gently/gradually fold the egg white mixture into the batter, while using a rubber spatula until combined.

5. Divide batter evenly between prepared pans, smoothing with an offset spatula. Bake until golden, about 30-35 minutes. Transfer pans to a cooling rack, and let cool completely for 1 hour. Invert cakes onto rack, peel off parchment, and reinvert cakes.

6. Using a serrated knife, trim tops of cake layers to make level. Place one layer on a serving plate, cut side up, and Place a large scoop of frosting and evenly spread over the top of the cake, gently place the second cake layer on top, cut side down, and frost. Next add the final layer of cake, cut side down. Spread entire cake with frosting, swirling to cover. Garnish cake atop with roses, and bottom of the cake with rose petals.

Quince Preserve

(Moraba'ye Beh

There is a hint of the days-gone-by in this sweet ruby red preserve. Enjoy for breakfast alongside feta cheese and barbari nan (thick Persian bread). This also makes for a lovely garnished atop of vanilla ice cream. Makes 3 Medium Size Jars

Ingredients

2 pounds quince
1 tsp. cardamom powder
1 tsp. cinnamon powder
1/2 cup raw organic honey
2 cinnamon sticks
2 whole green cardamom pods
1 cup water
1/2 cup rose water

Method

1. In a 6-quart saucepan boil water, and place canning jars, seals and lids into the water to be sterilize, drain and allow to dry.

2. Peel quince, cut each one in half and scoop out seeds.

3. Cut the quinces into 1/2-inch slices, and place in a bowl of cold water as you slice them, to prevent discoloration. Drain quince slices.

4. Place drained quince wedges in a heavy-bottomed medium saucepan on medium heat. Sprinkle with cardamom powder, cinnamon powder.

5. Add the cinnamon sticks, cardamom pods, water, honey, and rose water.

6. Cook the preserves for about 2 hours, stirring gently every 25 minutes, or until the liquid is reduced to a thick syrup, and the quinces have turned red. However, the quince wedges should still retain their shape. Remove from heat and allow to cool.

7. Fill the sterilized jars with the mixture, seal and store in a cool dark place.

*Note: If the syrup or compote begins to catch at the bottom of the pan, reduce the heat

Sour Cherry Preserve

(Moraba'ye Albalu)

This sweet and tangy cherry preserve is
traditionally served by some Sufis on Regaib kandili
the anniversary of the conception of the Prophet.
This sour cherry preserve is spooned into a warm
cup of tea, in means of symbolizing the bond
between this world, and the next.
Makes 3 Medium Size Jars

Ingredients:

3 pounds sour cherries
1 cup raw organic honey
2 oz. fresh lemon juice

Method:

1. In a 6-quart saucepan boil water, and place canning jars, seals and lids into the water to be sterilize, drain and allow to dry.

2. Remove stems from cherries, wash and drain, and pat dry with a towel. Place cherries on a clean cloth, and let cherries dry for 1-2 hours. Gently remove the pits of the cherries with a toothpick.

3. Place cherries, and honey into a large mixing bowl. Cover the bowl, and refrigerate overnight.

4. Place cherry mixture in a heavy-bottomed medium saucepan on medium heat, and add the lemon juice.

5. Cook the preserves for about 30 minutes, stirring gently every 10 minutes, or until the liquid is reduced to a thick syrup, add the lemon juice and let pan simmer for 5 additional minutes. Remove from heat and allow to cool.

6. Fill the sterilized jars with the mixture, seal and store in a cool dark place.

*Note: If the syrup or compote begins to catch at the bottom of the pan, reduce the heat

Rose Petal Preserves

(Moraba'ye Gol'e Sorkh)

This recipe for Moraba'ye gol'e Sorkh (rose petal preserves) is one of my most treasured recipes. This sweet and floral preserve is lovely with bread and warm tea, dolloped over yogurt, or served alongside plain white cake. In Unani medicine rose petal preserves are traditionally used as a cooling tonic to combat fatigue, lethargy, muscular aches, biliousness, itching, and heat-related conditions.

Ingredients

7 cups pink & red edible roses petals
2 cups water
1 cup raw organic honey
Juice from 2 lemons
4 tbsp. rose water

Method

1. In a 6-quart saucepan pot boil water, and place canning jars, seals and lids into the water to be sterilize, drain and allow to dry.

2. Rinse rose petals, drain with colander, and pat dry petals with a towel. Place dryed rose petals in a large mixing bowl, add half the honey, and the juice from 1 lemon. Cover the bowl, and refrigerate for 5 hour.

3. Place petal mixture in a heavy-bottomed medium saucepan over medium heat, and 2 cups water, and the remanding honey, and lemon juice.

4. Bring to a boil, and let simmer for 15 minutes, stirring gently from time to time.

5. Add rose water and let simmer for 2 minutes. Remove from heat and allow to cool.

6. Fill the sterilized jars with the mixture, seal and store in a cool dark place.

*Note: If the syrup or compote begins to catch at the bottom of the pan, reduce the heat.

Persian Trail Mix
(Ajeel)

Ajil is a medley of dried fruits, roasted nuts, and sometimes features little luxuries such as Rahat al-holqum (Turkish delight). Ajil is a staple in most Persian households, and is always offered to guest along side chai (tea). There are many variants for preparing Ajil - with endless variations. I have included two of my favorite ajil mixtures. However, feel free to have fun, and create your own signature mixture.

Ingredients

Sweet Trail Mix (Ajeel'e Shirin)
When making sweet trail mix only use unsalted nuts.
3 cups roasted pistachios
1 cup roasted chickpeas
1/4 cup medjool dates, pitted
1/4 cup dried apricots
1/4 cup dried cherries
1/4 cup dried mulberries
1/4 cup sugar-coated slivered almonds (noghl)
2 oz. Turkish delight (Rahat al-holqum)

Salty Trail Mix (Ajeel'e Shoor)
When making salty trail mix only use salted nuts.
2 cups roasted salted pistachios
1/2 cup dried cranberries
1/2 cup dried shirazi figs
1/4 cup dried apricots
1/4 cup dried grapefruit

Method

1. In a medium mixing bowl place all ingredients for your chosen ajeel mix, and mix ingredients together until incorporated.

2. Transfer nut mixture to a serving bowl, and enjoy.

Pomegranate Marinated Olives

(Zeytoon Parvardeh)

Olives marinated in pomegranate molasses - enough said! This wonderful combination is pure decadence. This recipe comes from the northern Caspian Sea, and is traditionally made with walnuts. Nevertheless it is also lovely when made with pistachios.

Serves 4

Ingredients

1/2 cup kalamata olives, pitted
1/2 cup green olives, pitted
1/4 cup pistachios or, walnuts
3 tbsp. extra-virgin olive oil
1/4 cup fresh mint, finely chopped
2 tbsp. pomegranate molasses
1 tbsp. raw organic honey

Garnish:
1/4 cup pomegranate arils

Method

1. In a large mixing bowl place olives, grated pistachios, extra-virgin olive oil, chopped mint, pomegranate molasses, honey, and mix together with a wooden spoon until incorporated. Place in an airtight container, and let marinate in the refrigerator for at least 24, preferable 48 hours.

2. To serve: place in a serving bowl, and sprinkle with pomegranate arils. Serve with Feta, and bread.

Dates Stuffed with Feta

(Mezze'e Khorma)

Indulgence is exactly the word that comes to mind, when I think of these little gems. Stuffed chewy dates with French feta, and a drizzle of honey is pure all-encompassing bliss.

Make 14 dates

Ingredients:

14 Medjool dates, cleaned, pitted, & scored down the middle
1/2 pond French feta

Garnish:
Drizzle of honey
Sprinkle of cinnamon powder
14 dried orange peels

Method:

1. In a medium mixing bowl place feta, and crumble feta with a wood spoon.

2. Stuff each date with 1 tablespoon of crumbled feta. Place dates on serving tray, garnish dates with a drizzle of honey, sprinkle a pinch of cinnamon powder, and top with dried orange peels.

Stuffed Grape Leaves
(Dolmeh)

A Persian dinner party would not be a Persian dinner party without stuffed grape leaves, and make for the perfect Vegan Mezze. Serve Warm or chilled.
Serves 4

Ingredients

1 Jar pickled grape leaves
2 cups long grain rice, soaked for 15 minutes, rinsed
1 cup chopped flat-leaf parsley
1 cup chopped tomato
1 ½ cup fresh lemon juice
1/2 cup extra-virgin olive oil
1/2 cup chopped yellow onion
½ tsp. cayenne pepper

1 tsp. salt
1/2 tsp. dried mint
1 pinch ground cinnamon

Garnish:
Lemon zest

Method

1. Soak vine lines in water to remove saltiness. Separate leaves and set aside unusable ones.

2. Drain rice, in a medium mixing bowl place rice, parsley, tomato's, ½ cup lemon juice, salt, dried mint, and cinnamon. Mix thoroughly.

3. To roll Dolmeh: Place 1 vine leaf rough side up, remove stem. Place 1 teaspoon of the mixture in the center near the base of the leaf. Fold the stem end over to cover the filling, fold both sides inward lengthwise and then firmly but not to tightly roll grape leaf. Repeat with the remaining leaves and filling.

4. Line an 8–quart saucepan with broken or unusable vine leaves. Place rolled grape leaves on top steam side down, lining from the outside in, so that they are tightly packed. Place a plate on top of the grape leaves, and on top on the plate place a clean heavy rock (this allows the dolma to keep their shape when cooking).

5. Place inside saucepan 1 cup lemon juice, and 1 cup of water, cover with the lid, and bring to a boil over medium high heat. Once at a boil reduce heat to medium low cook for 1 hour.

6. Once dolmas have cooked for an hour add ½ cup extra virgin olive oil, continue cooking for another hour.

7. Remove dolmas from stove, replace plate, leave untouched, and place saucepan in the refrigerator overnight.

Barbari Bread

(Nan'e Barbari)

Barbari bread is a thicker oval-shaped bread, much like focaccia, that is spinkled with sesame seeds. Barbari Bread is from Tabriz the Capital of East Azerbaijan province of Iran. This bread is also known as Nan'e Tabrizi. This bread is usually eaten for breakfast. Nevertheless, in my home we enjoy it with all meals.

Makes 3 loaves

Ingredients

1 package active dry yeast
1/2 cup warm water
1 tbsp. sugar
6 cups all-purpose flour, sifted
2 cups warm water
1 tsp. salt
1 tsp. baking powder

Glaze and Garnish:
A drizzle of extra-virgin olive oil
2 tbsp. nigella seeds or sesame seed

Method

1. In a medium mixing bowl, place yeast, sugar and warm water. Cover with plastic wrap and set aside for 10 minutes.

2. In a large mixing bowl place yeast mixture, warm water, salt, and gradually add 4 cups flour while constantly mixing mixture with your hands until a smooth elastic dough is formed (about 15 minutes). Shape dough into a ball, and place dough in a bowl oiled with extra-virgin olive oil. Cover bowl with plastic wrap. Set aside and allow dough to rise for 2 hours at room temperature.

3. Adjust oven rack to the middle position, preheat oven to 375° F, and Line three rimless baking sheet with parchment paper, or a non-stick baking mat.

4. Punch down the dough while still in the bowl. Place dough on a floured surface and knead for 10 minutes. Divide the dough into three balls of equal size. Place each dough ball on to onto the prepared baking sheets. With an oiled rolling pin, roll each dough ball out to a 14"x8" inch oval shape. With your fingertips make several long dents into the dough.

5. Drizzle the top of each loaf with extra-virgin olive oil, and sprinkle with nigella seeds or sesame seeds. Let loaves rest for 10 minutes before placing into preheated oven.

6. Bake for 20 minutes, then turn over and bake for an additional 10 minutes, and repeat this process for remaining dough. Serve warm.

Aromatic Herb Salad
(Sabzi Khordan)
Sabzi khordan or "eating greens" is a term given to fresh herbs that complements most Persian dishes, and is a lively alternative to the basic green salad.
Serves 4

Ingredients

1 bunch cilantro (ghishniz)
1 bunch flat-leaf parsley (jafari)
1 bunch fresh mint (Na'na)
1 bunch fresh spring onion (piazche)
1 bunch sweet basil (reyhan)
1 bunch watercress (sha'ahi)
1 bunch fresh radish (toropche)

Method

1. Simply remove stems from the cilantro, flat-leaf parsley, mint, sweet basil and watercress. Remove the green parts of the spring onions (you may serve them if desired). Wash herbs thoroughly in cold water, and pat dry with a clean tea towel.

2. To make radish rose garnish: Remove the leaves from the radish, clean, and cut off the radish roots and stems. With a paring knife slice four slices down each side of the radish, spacing slices evenly around the radish, make an additional four slices behind the first set of slices. Place radish in a bowl of ice water for 10 minutes, this allows the petals of the radish to open. Continue this process for the rest of the radishes. Place herbs on a platter, garnish with radish roses, and serve

Variation:
Nan'o Panir'o Sabzi: to the following above add lavash, feta cheese and walnuts, in addition you may warp the ingredients in the lavash for a tasty snack. This is a traditional dish served at a Persian wedding during the Sofreh Aghd.

Yogurt & Cucumber Starter
(Mast'o Khiar)

Persians have been partial to this dish since the 11th century, the combination of creamy yogurt, cool cucumber, onions, and mint is just divine.

Serves 4

Ingredients

4 Persian cucumbers, or 1 long English cucumber, peeled, finely chopped
1 small onion, finely chopped
2 cloves garlic, peeled, pressed
2 cup thick yogurt (Mast'e kisseh, lebne or Greek yogurt)
1 tbsp. lemon juice

2 tsp. dried mint
1/2 tsp. sea salt
1/2 tsp. freshly ground black pepper

Garnish:
2 tbls. dried rose petals

Method

1. In a serving bowl, mix all ingredients together. Cover and refrigerate for 1 hour before serving.

2. Garnish with rose petals, and serve as an appetizer with lavash.

Farmer's Cheese

(Panir

Panir is a very delicate, mild-tasting cheese, delicious with barbari and tea, and is also delightful as a appetizer with fresh herbs.

Serves 4-6

Ingredients

8 cups milk
1 cup yogurt at room temperature
3 tbsp. white vinegar

Method

1. Line a large colander with a large double layer of cheesecloth, and set it in your sink.

2. In a large wide pot, bring the milk to a gentle boil over medium heat, stirring frequently with a wooden spoon to avoid burning. Add the yogurt and vinegar and turn the heat down to low. Stirring gently, you should almost immediately see the curds (white milk solids) and whey (the greenish liquid) separate.

3. Note: If the milk doesn't separate add another tablespoon or two of vinegar. Stir in a motion that gathers the curds together rather than breaks them up.

4. Remove the pan from the heat and carefully pour the contents into the cheesecloth-lined colander. Gently rinse with cool water to get rid of the vingar flavor. At this point, you could squeeze out some of the liquid, and serve with honey, and some pistachios, almost like a fresh ricotta!

5. Next grab the ends of the cheesecloth and twist the ball of cheese to squeeze out the excess whey. Tie the cheesecloth to your kitchen faucet and allow the cheese to drain for about 5 minutes.

6. Twisting the ball to compact the cheese into a block, place it on a plate with the twisted part of the cheesecloth on the side, and set another plate on top. Weigh the second plate down with a heavy pot. Move to the refrigerator and let it sit about 15-20 minutes. Serve with Nan'e Barbari and tea.

Mamani's Spicy Feta

(Panir Mamani)

This spicy dip is quite addictive, and in my household disappears the minute it's made. This is technically not a Persian dish. However, a creation of my Mamani (Grandmother) who would make this for me since I'm a lover of spicy foods.

Serves 4

Ingredients

1 Pond feta, rinsed
1 red pepper, rinsed, unpeeled
2 cloves garlic, peeled
1 tsp. cayenne pepper
1/4 cup extra-virgin olive oil
4 tsp. fresh lemon juice
Salt and pepper to taste

Garnish:
Drizzle of extra-virgin olive oil
Sprinkle of cayenne pepper

Method

1. Preheat over to 400 °F.

2. Place the red pepper, and garlic on a rimmed baking sheet lined with parchment paper, prick the red peppers with a fork, and drizzle the red peppers, and garlic with olive oil, and a pinch of salt. Bake the garlic for 15 minutes, and remove from the oven, and set aside. Bake the red peppers for 30-40 minutes (turning them over twice during roasting), or until the skins are completely wrinkled, and lightly charred.

3. Remove red peppers from oven, and set aside until cool enough to handle (about 30 minutes). Remove the steam, skin and seeds, from the peppers, and cut them into quarters. Next pat dry the peppers with a paper towel. Discard the stems, peels, and seeds.

4. Into a food processor place feta, roasted peppers, roasted garlic, cayenne pepper, extra-virgin olive oil, and lemon juice. Blend until smooth. Salt and pepper to taste.

5. Place Spicy Feta on a serving plate. Garnish with a drizzle of extra-virgin olive oil and sprinkle with cayenne pepper.

Tomato & Cucumber Salad

(Salad'e Shirazi)

This light refreshing and aromatic salad is from Shiraz the capital of Fars Province part of Iran. This salad is a great everyday salad, and pairs well with many dishes.

Serves 4-6

Ingredients

Salad:
4 Persian cucumbers (or 2 seedless English cucumbers)
4 medium tomatoes, chopped into 1/2 inch cubes
1/2 medium red onion, finely chopped
1/2 cup fresh mint, roughly chopped

Dressing:
2 lemons, juiced
2 tbsp. grape seed oil
1/2 tsp. sea salt
1/2 tsp. freshly ground black pepper
Garnish:
1/4 cup fresh mint, chopped

Method

1. In a medium mixing bowl place lemon juice, grape seed oil, sea salt, and freshly ground black pepper. Whisk ingredients together.

2. In a serving bowl place cucumbers, tomatoes, red onions, fresh mint, and mix ingredient together. Pour dressing into the bowl, and toss the salad. Refrigerate for 2 hours before serving.

3. To serve garnish salad with fresh mint atop.

Watermelon, Rose Water Salad

(Salad'e Hendevaneh Va Panir

I simply love salty-sweet combinations, and this salad is a great play on both flavors. I love making this salad for picnics, and garden parties.

Serves 4-6

Ingredients

Salad:
1/2 of seedless watermelon, rind removed, cut into cubes
1/4 cup fresh mint, chopped
1/2 pound feta, cut into cubes

Dressing:
2 lemons, juiced
1/4 cup rose water
1 tsp. extra-virgin olive oil

Method

1. To make dressing, in a small mixing bowl place lemon juice, rose water, and extra-virgin olive oil. Whisk ingredients together.

2. In a serving bowl place watermelon cubes, chopped mint, feta cubes, and mix ingredient together. Pour dressing into the bowl, and toss the salad. Refrigerate for 2 hours before serving.

3. Serve chilled, garnish salad with fresh mint atop.

Chapter 9:
Tea Menus

Breakfast tea

Classic Persian Tea (Page 60)

Barbari Bread (Page 178)

Farmer's Cheese (Page 184)

Sour Cherry Preserves (Page 169)

Mehmooni
(Party)

Rock & Roll Chai (Page 98)

Gypsy Tea (Page 122)

Yogurt & Cucumber Starter
(Page 182)

Spicy Feta Dip (Page 186)

Stuffed Grape Leaves (Page 176)

Summer tea

Just Peachy Tea (Page 104)

Enlighten Mint tea (Page 80)

Aromatic Herb Starter
(Page 180)

Watermelon, Rose Water Salad
(Page 190)

Aroosi
(Wedding party)

Aroosi Tea (Page 88)

Rumi Tea (Page 94)

Persian Trail Mix (Page 172)

Dainty Sugared Almonds
(Page 160)

Star Cake (Page 166)

Recipes are listed in Farsi and English in alphabetial order; Recipes are also listed by English name under headings such as Sweets, Savory, etc.

Bibliography

Null, Gary. *The Complete Guide to Health and Nutrition.* New York: Dell, 1984
Ahmad, Jamil. A*hmad Unani: The Science of Graeco Arabic Medicine.* Indian: Roli Books Pvt Ltd, 1998
Ukers, William H. *The Romance of Tea.* Alfred A. Knopf. New York: 1936.
Cousi, Jean Pierre. *Food is Medicine.* Duncan Baird. London: 2001.

For the love
of tea.